Taming Your Wild Child:

7 Proven Principles for Raising Connected and Confident Children

By Tangee Veloso

An imprint of Zenrika Publishing

Copyright © 2013 and 2016 by Tangee Veloso.

All rights reserved worldwide.

No part of this document or the related files may be reproduced or transmitted in any form, by any means (electronic, photocopying, recording, or otherwise) without the prior written permission of the publisher.

ISBN 978-0-9985471-0-7

Edited by Tiffany Avans

Cover design: Dmitriy Konyushenko

Cover photo: Tiberon Tramblie

This book is dedicated to Michelle Barone who was an extraordinary family therapist and parent educator/natural learning consultant. She was a Certified Neuro Emotional Technique practitioner and a Diplomat in Comprehensive Energy Psychology. She weaved her knowledge and experience together to support and facilitate change and growth in mind, body, and spirit.

Michelle was the founder of "The Unschooling Summit" and the "Finding Your Way: Unlimited Possibilities in A Natural Learning Lifestyle" community. She wrote the book, "Finding Your Way: Exploring Your Families Educational Journey."

She was a special woman whose purpose here was to be of service and had truly helped to heal and transform her client's life wounds so they could create the lives that they wanted. Her nurturing and humorous nature was ingrained in every fiber of her being.

She was an uplifting mentor in the homeschooling, La Leche League, and conscious parenting communities. She was such an inspiration to many. She was a guest speaker for my organization, Family Love Village (FLV) and was a guest expert author whose articles were featured in our FLV newsletter, The FLVillage Crier.

Her expertise and warmth had gifted my family her wisdom on topics that my family values. She not only was our therapist, she was our friend. As my son's dad, Dalmacio said, *"She could see through your bullshit and call you on it!"* Yet it was always in the most loving and conscious way!

You will be deeply missed. And in honor of all that you have done in so many communities, this book is in dedication to you my friend. I love you.

CONTENTS

INTRODUCTION 1

CHAPTER ONE:
What Does Neuroscience Have to Do with Parenting, Anyway? 5

CHAPTER TWO:
How Does Trauma Affect the Family Dynamic? 12

CHAPTER THREE:
Time-Outs, Bribes & Good Jobs! Do They Really Work? 23

CHAPTER FOUR:
What Is the Key to Creating Quality Relationships in Your Family? ... 42

CHAPTER FIVE:
What is Conscious Parenting? 58

CHAPTER SIX:
What is the Triad of Connection? 64

CHAPTER SEVEN:
Why is Validation So Vital? 76

CHAPTER EIGHT:
From Caterpillar to Butterfly: What Helps Through Transitions? 88

CHAPTER NINE:
Is It Possible to Set Boundaries That Inspire Connection? 101

CHAPTER TEN:
What's That Feeling in Your Gut? 120

CHAPTER ELEVEN:
What is the Secret to Taming Your Inner Wild Child So That
Your Buttons Don't Get Pushed (As Much)? 128

CHAPTER TWELVE:
Does It Take a Village to Raise a Conscious Parent? 146

EPILOGUE 154

IT TRULY DOES TAKE A VILLAGE 159

INDEX 164

REFERENCES 166

ABOUT THE AUTHOR 170

INTRODUCTION

Do you ever have a gut feeling that there has to be a better way to connect with your child, but you don't have the resources or support to do so?

Do you feel you're constantly battling with your children and running out of ideas on how to find peace within the home?

Have you noticed that, perhaps, the parenting methods you are using just aren't working and you're feeling completely frustrated a majority of the time?

When our children are first born, we are moved to tears of sheer bliss as we cuddle them in our arms. We are in awe and amazement with how we are able to bring such beautiful bundles of joy into the world. Then they start to grow up and the wonder turns into moments of fatigue and frustration as they test our limits and patience. They acquire a voice to share their strong opinions and suddenly the "overwhelm" of parenting, working, finances, and finding balance within the home weigh down upon us.

Raising a child is one of the most important, gratifying, yet challenging jobs we will ever have. When both parents and children are able to get their own needs met and are able to find tools, resources, and community to support them, it can pave the pathway to more harmonious moments in the home. Yet, it's not always easy getting there! And when parents don't have the tools and support needed, this can create disconnection for the entire household.

As parents, we do our best with the knowledge we have; but what if what we don't know is really the issue at hand? People say, "ignorance is bliss." But what if our ignorance in wanting to learn another philosophy to parenting is getting in the way of our children thriving, including the relationship with our children? And if there is another way, what are the tools we can use to create a mutually respectful way to communicate with one another?

For most moms and dads, they tend to use what I like to call "Recycled Parenting Patterns." This is where parents feel that they aren't parenting as harshly as their parents did; but at some point begin to say, *"Oh my gosh–I've turned into my mom or dad!"* So when it comes to wanting to find another solution that can create connection, sometimes it is hard to navigate with which ones resonate with your family dynamic. With so many different styles and techniques out there, it can be challenging to choose.

In this book, I will share the 7 Proven Principles, along with resources that can help to get you started. I have been implementing these conscious tools for the past nine years. And even though my son is only eight years old, I have been practicing some of them since he was a little zygote in my tummy.

How I got started on this path with conscious parenting all began with the desire to give my son the best experience of thriving, and not merely surviving, in the world. Over the course of my pregnancy, I became hyper-sensitive to disconnection being a frequent occurrence within families. I felt there had to be another way to communicate with our loved ones. I soon started researching for resources and was led to a book called Connection Parenting – Parenting Through Connection Instead of Coercion, Through Love Instead of Fear by Pam Leo. I was so inspired by Pam's message, I reached out to my family and friends who had children and created my own workshop around this book.

What started out as an intimate group of families coming together to explore new and better ways to parent, evolved into a heart-centered community. Family Love Village (FLV), was a place where families could commune and delve into the beautiful yet messy world of parenting. We led monthly potluck gatherings where we had (and continue to have) a medley of guest speakers that come to our village to share their wealth of wisdom, as well as other workshops and resources. Families are able to learn many philosophies and techniques that allow the parents and caregivers the courage to guide their children in becoming confident and compassionate human beings, while simultaneously nurturing cooperation within the whole household.

Back to the 7 Proven Principles of this book. Even though the title of my book is called Taming Your Wild Child, it is not really so much about making your overzealous kid calmer. Trust me, I probably have one of the wildest ones out there (some say he's got the energy of two or three kids all in one)! If we are being honest, there have definitely been moments where I just wanted to tame his behavior (er...strangle him...ahem), but I know deep down inside that it's really about how I am reacting to his behavior that is causing me to want to pull my hair out!

Most parents feel that it's the behavior that needs to be addressed, but really it's not a child's behavior that is the root cause of their actions, it's the disconnection and unmet needs that are the catalyst. So this book won't be giving you tips on how to make your child "behave" (there's enough of that going around). It is really about the wild child within YOU that you will be learning how to tame, along with cultivating the 7 Proven Principles that can create a more loving partnership with your children - especially in the midst of the oh-so challenging moments!

When you are able to do the little things that create connection with your child consistently and are able to hone in on the 7 Proven Principles, you will be able to feel more <u>confident</u> in your parenting techniques and become more <u>compassionate</u> towards your children (as well as yourself–especially when you fall back into old parenting habits). Suddenly you will begin to notice that your children will also reflect the same confidence and compassion towards themselves and others, and that will organically transform who they are being in the world.

<u>The lenses through which we see our children affect our ability to integrate the tools in a meaningful way.</u> Once you're able to weave the principles into your life as a daily practice AND tap into your own well of intuition, <u>transformation takes place!</u>

You will learn from this book:

- What it means to be a conscious parent in your own home and how to become aware of your choices

- The seven principles that can build a deeper connection with your child

- How to set loving boundaries without losing your cool

- Techniques that honor self-care and self-love so that you can become more present with your parenting choices

- Why it is so important to find your own village to cultivate connection amongst other parents and caregivers on this same parenting journey

- And much more!

I promise if you actually take the time to read this book, I'm going to save you time with having to research on your own for ways that naturally transform your child's behavior and create a truly deeper connection with him/her. You will receive nuggets of insight within the pages of this book that will give you relief, comfort, and support. I will give you everything I know, but my request is that you take action on your part and read this book!

As it once was said, *"It's not what you know, it's what you do with what you know."*

So let's not confuse the thought of motion with the <u>act</u> of motion.

Are you ready to take action? Are you ready to tame that wild child within yourself in order to listen to your intuition and find new possibilities of parenting to create connection, confidence, compassion, and cooperation? The time is NOW to turn the page and begin a new chapter within your family's home.

CHAPTER ONE:
What Does Neuroscience Have to Do with Parenting, Anyway?

"A man paints with his brains and not with his hands, and if he cannot have his brains clear he will come to grief."
~ Michelangelo

Have you ever wondered why it is so difficult for your child to listen when they are upset? Do you sometimes feel you're repeating yourself over and over again?

Metaphorically speaking, Michelangelo's quote has much truth in it - especially when it comes to our children. When our children are experiencing a rush of flooded feelings, it is difficult for them to think clearly (or as in the case of the artist, to create clearly).

I have been on this path of parenting through connection ever since my son was in the womb and I find it fascinating how the brain works in relation to how neurons connect. Another aspect of connection is understanding how neurons work and our children's ability to learn or not learn under distress.

In this chapter, we will discuss:

- How the brain works in relation to your child's development

- The four main emotions and where they come from

- What emotional intelligence means and why it is so important

- Ways to help parents become more aware and understanding of their children's behavior

Once you've read this chapter you will have a clearer picture of neuroscience, emotional intelligence, what they have in common and why it all plays an important role in parenting.

So turn the page and discover why neuroscience and becoming aware of your child's emotions is key in creating a harmonious relationship with your child.

Did you know that humans are born without fully developed brains? The rest of our organs, though small, are fully developed. And even though most of the development occurs between birth and age ten, the brain doesn't fully mature until our early twenties!

Do you know what that means? It means that the brain's critical part of decision-making, problem solving, and reasoning (a.k.a. the prefrontal cortex) usually develops by age 25. Yet in our society, at the age of 18, one is considered an adult and given privileges and responsibilities, such as voting or enlisting in the army.

When I was 18 years old, my mom decided to move near San Diego, CA and asked if I wanted to move with her. Because I was "in love" at the time (and also couldn't wait to be on my own), I chose to stay behind in Los Angeles and thus began my adulthood. I do have to say there were definitely some poor choices that I made for myself back then. Perhaps it could've been the rebellious streak coming out, finally, after so many years of being restricted from doing fun things (a.k.a. being grounded all the time) and discovering myself freely.

I found it quite interesting to learn that statistics say that because an adolescent's prefrontal cortex is only partway through the process of being fully developed, the ability to plan and organize can sometimes be a bit of a challenge for a typical 18-year-old.

Here's an interesting fact: babies are born with one billion neurons in their brain. Talk about fascinating! If you think about it, that is probably as many stars as there are in the Milky Way. And because neurons are not yet connected at birth, brain development is all about growing connections or circuits between neurons. How neurons get connected and how strong the circuits get "wired" has to do with emotions. By age three, the weakest connections start to dissipate, while a connection that is used repeatedly in the early years remains permanent.

For instance, if a child is experiencing a continuous, positive experience with playing a family board game, the neuron connection with that will remain permanent. The same goes for a negative experience of the child witnessing her parents arguing all the time.

Statistics state that when young children are exposed to continuous stress, negative parenting, an unhealthy diet and various other environmental issues, it can have adverse long-term effects on health and emotional wellness as an adult. One solution for moving through negative experiences is to introduce preventative actions. This is exactly where this book comes into place for parents wanting to learn these preventative tools, as well as continuous skills for every stage of development, which will help build a strong connection between the parent and the child.

Research has shown there are four basic emotions universally experienced. They are happiness/joy, sadness, fear/shock, and anger/disgust.

To fully understand why children's emotions and feelings can sometimes bring up "unwanted behavior," it's essential to understand where these emotions come from and how the brain works.

So where do these emotions come from?

Emotions activate in the brain, specifically in the limbic system, which is located in the middle of the brain. An important component to learning is our memory, which involves the limbic system. Think of the limbic system as the mediator between thoughts and feelings – it translates and directs emotions and behavior. Thus, why emotions play an important role in making good decisions and being able to think clearly (similar point to what I interpreted with Michelangelo's quote in the beginning of this chapter).

Priscilla Vail, author of Emotion: The On/Off Switch For Learning, best describes a great analogy for this. She explains how the emotions are like an off and on switch to learning. So when a child feels joy and reassurance, she is able to connect, learn, and create more freely

– hence her switch is on. But when she is upset, feels threatened or loses her sense of connection, it is hard for her to focus–especially under continuous emotional distress, which can actually stifle her ability to learn – hence her switch being off. It is during these stressful times that her prefrontal cortex tends to shut down. Consequently, it can be frustrating and confusing at times for children when an adult says, "use your words," because when they are in that moment of angst and upset, it is difficult for them to form their feelings into words. If you think about it, when was the last time you (with your fully developed brain) were able to learn or remember something when you were scared, mad, or depressed? Now put yourself in your child's shoes, with her not-so-fully-developed brain, and imagine how she must feel whenever these emotions arise? A lot of frustration can erupt, including unresolved past feelings that may surface.

Ah yes! Unresolved past feelings - that is a key term that I would like to discuss in more detail here. So many times, unresolved, past feelings can go unnoticed. When a child has not been able to release their flooded feelings in a healthy manner from a previous upset (i.e. allowed to cry or rage - again in a healthy way), more than likely, his emotions can begin to build throughout the day. And before you know it, what was once a peaceful child playing just before dinner is now upset at the table for something as simple as forgetting to give him his favorite sippy cup. Even unresolved feelings from the day before can trickle into the following day's activities. Say for instance, your child witnesses you and your spouse arguing the day before; even though your child also observed the two of you resolving things from the argument and all seemed well towards the end of the night, he could experience big feelings throughout the next day, as he releases and tries to work through his feelings.

Unfortunately, this behavior gets labeled as "tantrums, terrible twos or manipulative." Of course, now given the knowledge that children's brains are still in the development stage until their mid-twenties, perhaps this can help make it easier to become more compassionate rather than labeling the behavior in such a manner. Unfortunately in most cases, adults that aren't aware of this tend to punish the child by sending him to his room or the "naughty chair," when in reality, what he needs is connection with a loved one, not to be isolated to deal with his feelings alone. In most cases, parents put children in a "time out" or the "naughty chair" due to something that they did "wrong" but in most cases, children aren't thinking of what they did "wrong". They very well may be thinking of how to not get caught the next time or unfortunately, sometimes may be thinking of how to get even (especially if there is a sibling involved). And the most important thing that is happening here is what I mentioned above: feeling alone and disconnected. If you really think about it, the message that parents are sending to their child, when they send him away, is that they can't handle his emotions or the situation. Eventually that child is apt to stop coming to a parent with his issues or might hide his feelings out of fear of being rejected. As he grows older, what could result from being continuously shunned away via the "naughty chair" is the possibility of this child turning to outside influences, such as peer pressure, by using some form of substance to numb his emotions.

Here's a great example of how one's prefrontal cortex can shut down in the midst of frustration and disconnection. When I was about 15 years old, my mom's boyfriend at the time would try and help me with my homework–more like intimidate me, actually. At the time, I was having difficulty understanding math word problems. Instead of being encouraged in a loving and supportive way, I was called names like "stupid" and belittled with statements like *"Can't you figure this out already?"* Obviously, my brain switched off each time this happened, and the memory of this experience continued to create a negative impact with learning whenever he tried helping me with homework. Even up to this day, whenever I feel insecure or threatened with confrontation, I start to notice myself getting nervous while trying to explain something.

Now that happened to me when I was a teenager. Can you imagine how much more challenging it can be for a child, whose circuitry is still forming, to be able to learn when an adult scolds them? Especially when in the throes of big feelings, it can be a struggle to register words or language and might actually seem as if we are speaking a foreign language.

We've talked about the brain, emotions that stem from the brain, as well as the limbic system, prefrontal cortex and the effects that emotions can have on the inability to learn. There's one more key element to a child's development and that is Emotional Intelligence.

Emotional Intelligence or EQ is the ability to have self-awareness, self-regulation, motivation, empathy, and socials skills. These five components of EQ, when practiced daily, can help someone move through stress, overcome challenges and defuse disagreements with more ease while being able to communicate effectively with compassion. Where IQ can determine someone's intellectual ability, EQ is important for helping to manage a person's emotions and improving their relationships. So if our goal is to raise happy, confident, resilient, and compassionate adults who are successful and fulfilled in life, then EQ is a vital key towards that vision for our children.

When we're talking about a child's EQ, it is important to guide her in finding ways to identify her feelings and be able to regulate her impulses in a healthy and productive way.

A few suggestions would be:

- *Accept your child's emotions.* An example of what to say when he's mad would be: *"That must've been frustrating."*

- *Help your child label the emotion.* For example, *"I'm noticing you're upset."*

- *Encourage him to express his feelings* by asking, *"How did that make you feel?"*

When it comes to neuroscience and parenting, it is such a vital factor in being able to understand how the two relate to one another. So now that you have a bit more understanding about how the brain works, how children's emotions can affect their learning and the importance of emotional intelligence, perhaps your awareness can shed some light on the importance of being more conscious and empathetic when your child gets flooded with feelings.

Tangee Veloso

In the following chapter, we will go over how to identify trauma and how trauma can affect your child's development. This is an important topic, as trauma can sometimes be overlooked - you'd be surprised at the levels of traumatizing events that can affect how you connect with your child.

Chapter Two:
How Does Trauma Affect the Family Dynamic?

"Time may heal physical pain but only love can heal emotional pain."
~ Amir Zoghi

In the very first chapter, we discussed the importance of how the brain works in relation to your child's development. Now we will talk about trauma and how it relates to your growing child.

We hear the word trauma and we think, *"Oh no! Not my child."* Yet, did you know that more than two thirds of today's children have experienced and/or witnessed a traumatic event by age 16?

In this chapter, we will address the following:

- Distinguishing between the various forms of trauma

- Effects of emotional trauma on the brain

- Easy-to-implement techniques for relieving and repairing trauma in children

So now that you have a clearer picture of what is going to be discussed in this chapter, read on to learn more about the many faces of trauma and how you can help your child through these traumatic experiences.

What defines trauma, you may ask? Trauma can come in many forms. The most common is physical, emotional, sexual, and/or medical. Most people, when they think of trauma, assume it has to be a severe experience. However, what can appear minuscule can actually be damaging to a child's development when it is repeated over time.

Trauma can take place not only within the home, it can also occur in public, in schools, and even in the womb or at birth. Once you understand what causes trauma and how to identify if your child has experienced it, you can help your child move through it.

Some examples of trauma that children can experience are: a bad injury from a fall or recurring medical issues, parental fighting/domestic violence, verbal abuse, lack of affection or love, divorce, violent media, instability in the home (moving from home to home), remarriage, getting accustomed to a new family or bullying from other kids, parents and/or caregivers.

Trauma can come in the form of belittling, degrading, and ridiculing. It can also come from making a child feel unsafe, including the threat of abandonment. Even time-outs or allowing your baby to "cry it out" can be considered traumatic experiences where a child can feel unloved, insecure, and unsupported.

Those mentioned above are more apparent causes of distress, but there are more subtle causes, too. One example of a less noticeable cause could be when you have a child that has a higher need to move their body but instead is expected to sit still for long periods of time in school or at home (which unfortunately can lead to children being labeled ADD/ADHD).

Another prevalent stressor is not being able to connect with nature. The importance of being in nature is often overlooked. And nature deficit can become detrimental to a child's development. In today's age, unfortunately, the natural environment has sadly declined as television, video games, demanding schoolwork, and technology continues to skyrocket. Even though evidence has shown that being outdoors relieves children who are highly stressed out, statistics continue to show more children are less in touch with Mother Earth.

So what happens when a child is highly stressed out? Stress and trauma can affect his or her ability to think and feel, which affects their behavior.

Several behaviors include:

- Delays in development
- The development of new fears
- Regressive behavior
- Separation anxiety (particularly in young children)
- Sleep disturbance, nightmares
- Feelings of depression; angst
- Feelings of blame and guilt
- Loss of interest in normal activities
- Reduced focus and possible decline in schoolwork
- Social withdrawal
- Anger, acting out
- Self-destructive behaviors
- Excessive somatic complaints of physical ailments

Emotional Trauma and Its Effect on the Brain

Are you familiar with the term "flight, fight, or freeze"? As mentioned in the first chapter, during a stressful event, the nervous system can turn the switch button off therefore activating the flight, fight, or freeze response.

Let me paint a picture for you on what can occur during a flight, fight or freeze scenario. Let's say there is a child on the swings in the playground and an older child comes over and starts bullying the first child. One option the first child might consider is running away, fleeing from the scene. Another option that could occur is the younger child might feel the urge to fight back; and the last option is he may become frozen, unable to move at all.

There is a stress hormone called cortisol that releases through the nervous system. When time heals and the stressor goes away, the nervous system responds and allows the body to return back to normal. However, if trauma is repeated or if extreme amounts of stress occur, excess cortisol gets released into the body. This large amount of cortisol can have negative effects on the brain and can actually damage neurons in the brain.

In deep-seated trauma, there could be triggers that continue to cycle and repeat themselves, sometimes surfacing years later. But with time, the trauma can subside when you consciously move through it. One tool that can help tremendously for adolescents and adults is journaling, suggested by my dear friend, Jennifer Kelly.

Jennifer Kelly (Owner of The Yogi Tree, a KRI Certified Kundalini Yoga Teacher, Khalsa Way Prenatal Teacher, Light Leader's Children's Yoga Teacher and SuperHealth as taught by Yogi Bhajan for Addiction Recovery Teacher, a Post Partum Doula, and Complete Wellness Specialist) has been studying the effects of trauma. She has seen first-hand how it can affect children through her experiences with her adopted sons, as well as being a foster parent for the past eleven years. Jennifer mentions that an effective journaling process includes recording the severity of the episodes, noting the recovery from each episode and how it can be reassuring to reflect back and see the progress that you are making. This can be a wonderful outlet for older children and teens.

But what about a child who isn't familiar with journaling and not able to take note of the episodes that occur? What if this technique isn't as desired by a younger mind, and what could possibly occur if a child doesn't know how to release the trauma in a healthy way?

Let's use the example above with a child being bullied by an older child as the traumatic experience. He/she can sometimes hold in the emotions only to "act out" later at home. Unfortunately, a child's reactions to traumatic events can be labeled and identified as behavioral issues that parents associate with the "terrible twos" or "growing pains."

As mentioned in the first chapter, when a child experiences continuous emotional distress, the prefrontal cortex tends to shut down. During this shutdown, and due to a lack of emotional maturity, a child finds it challenging to come up with the appropriate language and actions to express his emotions and feelings. And when he doesn't know how to express his feelings and emotions, more than likely, he will end up hitting, biting, and/or scratching. These actions are not meant to hurt anyone maliciously. And with a child still in the developing process, often the violent behavior is simply a form of release. He may become confused about the emotions he's feeling; and in order to get it out of his system, it may unwittingly come in the form of violent behavior.

Unlike an adult or teenager, recording the recovery progress might not be a child's first choice, so what are ways he/she can release the trauma?

Some creative ways to help a child through trauma, grief, loss, depression, anger, and anxiety are:

- Art
- Music
- Storytelling
- Creative writing
- Poetry
- Dance

Statistics show improvement with trauma when children are able to tap into creative tools to help alleviate stress. I have been dancing and writing poetry since I was nine years old. Reminiscing through the pages (especially throughout my teenage years), the words I have used to express my thoughts and feelings on paper have been extremely healing. The same has been true with dancing, as well.

In the past ten years, I had drifted away from writing spoken word and had tuned in to another outlet as a fire performer. Recently, though, I discovered that when I write spoken word, it is extremely more beneficial for moving through my emotions. Because I had stopped writing on a regular basis, my feelings were becoming numb, except for my anger.

When I was overly stressed, overwhelmed, and undernourished by not getting my needs met, I started noticing that I was becoming an angry person (specifically towards my husband at the time, unfortunately).

See how as an adult, when our needs are unmet and there isn't an appropriate release, our behavior can lash out at our loved ones? Now imagine you're just a toddler or even a teenager, and how it can be even more of a challenge to think straight, especially knowing that the brain doesn't fully develop until our early twenties.

Now after re-igniting the spark of my first love with writing, it has allowed me to tap into a wellspring of creativity that has actually transformed and transcended my emotions into a more elevated state of being. Thankfully, this too can become possible for children suffering from trauma.

Now that we have discussed positive solutions for children/teenagers, how about for pregnant moms and their unborn babies in the womb?

Earlier I shared that a stressful event during pregnancy and/or birth that is passed on from a mother to her unborn child is also considered traumatizing. When I was about six or seven months pregnant, my husband at the time and I were going through a bit of a rough transition in our lives. During that challenging time, our midwife, Elizabeth Bachner (Founder and Clinic Director of

Gracefull Birthing Center), had mentioned an amazing technique that could help as a preventative with trauma for the baby. Elizabeth shared the importance of early trauma resolution, which she had learned from Dr. Ray Castellino, the Director of Castellino Prenatal and Birth Therapy Training and co-founder of BEBA (Building and Enhancing Bonding and Attachment).

Since I was already on the path with learning about connection and creating a sacred environment to have a natural birth at home, it felt intuitively resonant to use this simple yet powerful technique that Elizabeth suggested. So whenever my son's dad and me would have a disagreement that caused stress on my end, I would take the time to connect with my baby. I would reassure him that what was happening between daddy and myself had nothing to do with him, that he didn't have to take on my feelings as his own.

And although I could not actually tell with hard evidence that what I was saying was effective, I intuitively could feel that it was helping! It was such a powerful tool that after our son was born, we continued to use this tool to reassure our son that our disagreements had nothing to do with him (and still continue to do up to this day).

I am not condoning arguing in front of your children, whatsoever, as this can cause trauma on many levels. But parents do argue (and most have done this in front of their children at one time or another).

There are two things that have remained important components of our family's philosophy, and I'd like to share them, as they could be helpful for others.

- We would gently let our son know that the arguments were never about him; that the arguments were about our own reactions and unmet needs.

- When we would make up, we always did our best to do this in front of our son.

It is crucial for children to know that they are not to blame for the adult disagreements, in order for them to not feel guilty or develop low self-esteem. And it is just as important for them to also experience seeing their parents make up after an argument in order to role model what it looks like to consciously re-connect and communicate in loving and respectful ways.

Another key element when it comes to childhood trauma is that when given a safe and supportive environment in which a child's needs are met physically and emotionally, the trauma can be healed with time. As long as there is a strong sense of connection being established between the child and an adult, the light at the end of the tunnel towards recovery can be reached.

As discussed in the first chapter, while the child is in that heightened state, they are in their lower brain. This part of the brain is all about survival. There is no logic or reason. You must help guide your child back to their higher brain through connection, before you can talk reason and logic.

I felt it was imperative to include this chapter in this book so that we, as parents, can become more aware of the various ways that trauma can surface and learn how we can become more supportive in helping our children move through the stress. In order for us to help our youth, repair early childhood damage and build more harmony and cooperation within our children, we must become more aware of our choices, as well as utilize a deep sense of understanding and empathy. And probably one of the most important things to remember in healing from trauma is that you can choose to move beyond the experience without becoming a victim of it; meaning it is something you move through and the experience does not have to define you.

In retrospect, if we are to lead the path for our children, one that imprints a conscious, loving, and compassionate livelihood for their upbringing, we must also know what is and isn't working in order to evolve.

And just as it is important to help children heal their trauma, it is imperative for us adults to heal our past trauma, as well. If you are not able to heal your past hurts, they will continue to trickle onto your children.

Chris Morasky, a wildlife biologist with 30 years of experience teaching Stone Age skills and nature connection and founder of Wisdom Keepers (nature classes for families based in Los Angeles and Oregon), shared his thoughts on trauma and an intriguing point of view about how our children's ability to push our buttons is a gift:

> *"Whatever traumas are not dealt with in childhood continue through adulthood, then through old age, and finally to death. Traumas that are not dealt with eventually are physically expressed as illness or injury and via a lower vitality (it is no coincidence that auto-immune diseases are steadily rising, partly due to this). And... you pass your traumas on to your children. The way this happens is fascinating and actually quite beautiful. Your child intuitively senses your traumas and unconsciously finds ways to engage your issues (we call this "pushing your buttons"). Nobody can push your buttons like your own child, right? THIS IS A GIFT. Remember, you can only let go of your limitations when your "stuff" is "up". Children are born to raise up their parents, not the other way around."*

Exercise:

Where could unhealed traumas affect your ability to connect with your children?

_____

_____

_____

_____

_____

_____

_____

When you feel triggered, where do you experience that feeling in your body? What quality does that experience have? Bring your awareness to these symptoms. For instance, do you notice tension in your body and if so, where? How is your breathing? Do you feel pain in your body (i.e. stomach cramps, headaches, etc). Write down a list of these symptoms.

Now that you have become aware of possible unhealed trauma, where in your body it may affect your well-being and have read some tools above that can help your child move through their trauma, what are ways that you can heal through your own? What are your passions? What do you love doing? How do you get to that place where you feel safe and the "fight, flight, or freeze" response is no longer a factor for you? Write down a list of what has helped you in the past and/or new ways that can help you regain confidence within you, as a person and as a parent.

_____

_____

_____

_____

_____

_____

_____

_____

_____

_____

_____

_____

_____

As eloquently stated by my friend and soul sister, Genesis Ripley, *"Exercises like these are a practice, that allow us to open a window to the dark corners of our unconscious. Our children, gift to us, these opportunities to uncover and work toward freeing ourselves from unconscious fear and belief. We often see parenting as something we do for our children. In connected parenting however, it is a sacred dance where parent and child can grow and heal together."*

So now that you know more about trauma and its effects on the development of your growing child, let's turn the page and find out why some of the parenting philosophies that we grew up with aren't as effective as we thought they would be.

Chapter Three:
Time-Outs, Bribes & Good Jobs! Do They Really Work?

"Love has its own time, its own season and its own reasons from coming and going. You cannot bribe it or coerce it or reason it into staying.
You can only embrace it when it arrives and give it away when it comes to you."
~ Kent Nerburn

So often parents think praise, rewards, and punishments work; yet, what is sometimes overlooked is that it only works for a short period of time and it does not allow a child to consider how his or her actions affect her experience. As children develop, self-love can become increasingly challenging to attain when this form of parenting is used. The end result can turn into disconnection and long-term adverse effects for emotional well-being in adulthood.

There are many aspects to this parenting style that create disconnection. Statistics show that the more recent advice from conventional books and experts suggesting techniques, such as timeouts with the "naughty chair" or even what is considered "positive" rewards for compliance, can be just as detrimental to the child's well-being as spanking or hitting.

Researchers are discovering that fear-based and intimidating parenting approaches merely give a short-term resolution. Like using a spare tire for your flat (as Pam Leo describes in her book), it is truly just a "quick fix" – a temporary compliance which can create disconnection and long-term harm to not only the parent/child bond but for the child's development, as well.

Authoritarian parenting has been in the forefront for many families, and recycled parenting patterns have inflicted disconnection for generations. The effects of trauma and disconnection that we had as children will reflect in the way we see and move through the world as adults. When these traumas are not recognized and given the opportunity and tools to heal, the patterns trickle down into how we parent our own children and the cycle continues.

Do you recall swearing to yourself that you would never be like your parents? Only to wake up one morning to the realization that you have indeed become your worst nightmare – you have become your parents! Does this sound familiar?

Okay, maybe not every person has disagreed with how they were parented and actually came from an unconditionally loving home; but more so than not, people have been raised in a somewhat dysfunctional upbringing.

In this chapter, I will highlight the following:

- Authoritarian parenting and why it doesn't work
- Disciplinary forms of control
- Permissive parenting and why it doesn't work
- Techniques that do work and examples to support it

To recap, we have learned in the previous pages that dysfunction can be caused by varying degrees of trepidation. Now we will go over what works and doesn't work with the varying degrees of parenting.

What is Authoritarian Parenting?

Authoritarian parenting (also considered traditional parenting) is a style that is based on strict discipline and a sense of "power over." It also tends to be manipulative and fear-based in its motives while relying on bribes, rewards and punishments. Its most concerning effect is that it compromises the connection between you and your child.

What is Coercive Control?

Coercive control is an attempt to influence the child, when the parent ends up taking advantage of the child's desire for love and approval. In other words, coercive control = authoritarian discipline.

Coercion can come in the form of:

- Blaming/guilting

- Shaming

- Withdrawing love

- Teasing in degrading ways

- Sarcasm or condescending remarks

- Invalidating feelings, thoughts or ideas

As mentioned above, rewards and punishments are another form of coercion.

The following are examples of rewards, punishments, and time-outs:

Example 1: REWARD - *"If you eat all your veggies, you can have dessert."*

Example 2: PUNISHMENT - *"If you don't eat all your veggies, you won't get dessert!"*

The first example uses bribery in order for the child to get the reward. The second one puts the child in a position where he is forced to do something in order to get something. Both are forms of trying to get your child to do what you want them to do and not necessarily about meeting his needs or creating a respectful relationship that honors authentic communication. Plus, you are inadvertently modeling manipulation to your child.

Solution for both: While making dinner, offer a couple of options for vegetables to see which one your child would like to eat. When you give children choices, it can help them feel a part of the process. Perhaps even ask them if they would like to prepare/cook the meal with you. Even going to the Farmer's Market together and getting to know the farmers or even growing your own garden are all great suggestions. Welcoming your child into the process of farming, growing and cooking meals together is a wonderful way for your child to explore different types of produce all the while building connection. And if they are still adamant about not wanting to try vegetables, perhaps prepare it in a different form, such as a smoothie. But the key here is to continue offering vegetables to your child without forcing it.

Example 3: TIME OUT - *"Go to your room and think about what you did to your sister!"* or *"Go to the naughty chair."*

Solution: Ah, the infamous "Time Out"! As challenging as it may seem in the midst of frustration on both parties, connection is what the child needs in these moments when he has done something "bad" or something of which parents don't approve.

Parents tend to think that putting their child in a time-out will make him think about what he did and realize the consequences. Yet when a child is in a time-out, he is not thinking of what he did "wrong." He is most likely feeling resentment, perhaps thinking of ways to get even. And the hardest part of what a child experiences during a time-out is feeling isolated from our love.

According to research, time-outs actually can damage the child's psyche and truthfully doesn't actually change the child's behavior. What it ends up doing is sending the child into a panic when we isolate him from our love. Again, this is where conditional parenting tends to "do to" the child instead of "working with" him/her.

It is imperative that we allow our children to experience their feelings - whether it is anger, aggression, and/or sadness that is in need of being expressed. If we are not able to support and encourage them to work through their feelings, then we are merely teaching them to sweep their feelings under the rug, so to speak. So, in terms of sending children into a time-out, it may seem like it works for the time being but the outcome of disconnection, separation and rejection (and perhaps the many years of therapy) just isn't worth it (at least in my eyes). Time-outs can also lead to our children shutting down and numbing their emotions, which can continue into their adulthood and influence how they communicate (or don't communicate) with others.

Another style of discipline is fear-based control. You know, the "Dont's," "No's," and "Be Careful's" that seem to roll off the tongue as fast as a semi-automatic. That's literally what it can feel like when kids are on the receiving end of our alarming and panicked commands.

Of course, it's only natural to want to protect our children from emotional harm and physical injury; but, when we're constantly instilling fear in what our children do, it can possibly:

- Make our children frightened of everything, which could numb their passion and creativity

- Startle our children and throw them off guard, so they accidentally do the very thing we are wanting them to be "careful of"

- Prompt them to explore the very thing that you continually are trying to prevent them from doing by saying the word 'don't' all the time

At times, this over-protectiveness can prevent a child from engaging in her world. Unfortunately, due to ingrained fear on the adult's part, a child may not see or fully experience it as her own world.

Additionally, they begin to not believe us when everything is a panic of a barked-out command. They lose trust in our ability to decide what is really true emergency from what is our personal emergency. If what they are doing is truly dangerous and unsafe, then that is a different story. In situations where it is truly dangerous, it's important that they see our authentic concern for their safety. But if they are always seeing that sort of response, they learn to not take it so seriously.

As adults, when we allow ourselves to experience new adventures and some risks, this frees up the space for us to explore our passions. The same can be said about our children, as well. Following our passions, whether as a child or an adult, can be the most empowering model of motivation that encourages confidence within. Although most parents want to see their children engage in their passions, it can sometimes be difficult to allow them to discover them on their own without interfering or imposing our own fears and opinions onto them.

Here are some examples of fear-based control and some solutions:

Example 1: *"Don't touch that!"*

When you say the word "don't" and attach a command after it, what they are hearing, most likely, is the command. If someone said to you, *"Don't look over there but....,"* what you tend to want to do is look. The same goes for children when you are telling them to not do something.

Solution: For babies/toddlers not yet verbal, saying *"Hot!"* instead of saying, *"Don't touch!"* is one way to express the warning without having to say "don't". Then let them know you're picking them up away from the stove and say, *"The stove is hot! You can't touch that but you can touch this,"* and give them something that they can touch (i.e. a toy). When we say adjectives, such as "hot," "sharp" or "danger," it gives a description of what the object is instead of constantly saying "don't" to your child.

So, instead of focusing on what you don't want your child to do, help them to engage in what you do want them to do. For older children, how about saying, *"Please keep your hands off"* instead of the infamous, *"Don't touch!"* You could say, *"Let's do this...,"* rather than *"Don't do that!"* and then proceed to show them what you would prefer them to do.

I had mentioned previously to let your child know when you are picking him/her up. Communicating to your child that you are picking him/her up, gives you another conscious tool with connecting in a respectful and loving way that lets your child know that you respect his/her body and autonomy.

If you are still wondering about this step, perhaps ask yourself this question: *"How would I feel if someone picked me up unexpectedly while I was focused on work or cooking dinner?"* If your answer is shocked, upset or uncomfortable, the same could be going through your child's mind - especially if he/she is absorbed in play, which in essence is his/her own work with learning.

FLV's very first guest speaker, Cody Dale, mentioned that during her RIE (Resources for Infant Educarer) training, they had a simulation course where the adults were attached to a bungee cord. They were put in a room where furniture and toys were oversized. The point of the course was for the trainees to understand what it is like to be a baby when an adult picks him/her up unannounced and interrupts their play. The students would be playing with objects and then suddenly out of nowhere would be lifted up via the bungee cord, giving the experience of what the baby must be feeling whenever picked up unexpectedly. I found the exercise intriguing and it really put into perspective how adults can unconsciously interrupt their children's world unintentionally. So ever since FLV's first workshop, I always announce to babies and toddlers when I am going to pick them up, so they know what to expect. In doing so, I have found that children respond more easily to this, as well.

Example 2: *"What is wrong with you? You could get run over by a car!"*

Solution: When the child/toddler is verbal, what could you do instead of scaring them into cooperating?

Let's say your child just tried crossing the street without looking. You remember to use the suggestion in Solution 1 by stating "Danger!" Now what? After assessing that the child is safe from harm, this is where you can learn to become a questioning parent and ask your child a question that helps him come up with his own solution that avoids scaring him into doing what you want him to do.

For instance, instead of saying "What is wrong with you? You could get run over by a car!" you could ask, *"Do you think it's safe to not look where you are going?"* and then await their answer. Then you could continue by asking, *"What do you think could happen?"*

You can also set a firm boundary by letting them know that you need to make sure their bodies are safe and need to hold hands.

Example 3: *"What are you doing?"* (in an upset or accusatory tone)

Solution: When children are constantly asked in a tone that sounds like you're already accusing them of doing something "wrong," it can lead to them feeling guilty and fearful of you. What would it take for you to be able to ask that very same question but in an inquisitive and gentle manner instead?

Whenever you ask your child vs. using fear as a way to control your child's response, it encourages her to come up with problem solving. It allows her to think about the issue and answer for herself. It also gives her the freedom to express what she is doing through her creative mind.

Which brings me to my next point: Always see the best intentions within your child! Unfortunately, adults tend to think the worst when it comes to what children are up to. But what if adults were to perceive children's actions differently? What if we could avoid reacting and assuming the worst by being inquisitive instead?

When we stop to really get present and come from a curious and speculative place instead of in reaction mode all the time with our children's actions, the innocence of their imagination can then be more understood and even supported rather than stifled and shunned. Therefore, it can become easier for us parents to empathize with their actions instead of engage in our own reactions.

The following is a great example from a five-year-old's point of view of what can occur when adults, unfortunately, do just the opposite and assume the worst:

My son and I had the wonderful opportunity to participate in an amazing home-schooling nature class with other families with children around the same age group. During one of the excursions, my son and his friends discovered a deep hole in the ground (perhaps a gopher's hole). The kids decided to gather rocks to cover it up. Instead of inquisitively asking what they were doing, I just assumed that they were trying to cover up the hole so that the gopher wouldn't get out.

Although I did inquire and ask them how they thought the animal might feel if it couldn't get out, I hadn't actually gone deeper to ask what their creative minds were doing. Even though, thankfully, we, as the parents, weren't reprimanding any of the children, we did automatically jump to the conclusion that they were trying to trap whatever animal might be living in there without being the slightest curious to know what their imaginations were stirring up.

Towards the end of the class, our nature guide had stated, *"When you hurt the animals and plants around us, it makes me see that you didn't think this through."* Although our nature mentor was doing his best to be gentle with his words, this statement had completely shifted the children's energy, and you could tell by their faces that they felt "bad" or "wrong."

Later on, during their bedtime story ritual, one of the moms asked her son how he felt about what happened during the nature class. The dialogue went something like this:

> *"Our instructor doesn't understand. Doesn't he know we were saving the planet from the bad guys hiding in the Cactus? They were everywhere and they were trying to steal all the life energy from our planet."*

Then the mom asked how her son felt about what the instructor had said at the end of class. Her son continued on to say:

> *"He was being very disrespectful. I had to defend us. We were all just so excited to be on that new land. It was amazing land! We all just wanted to play and have fun."*

The mom continued to ask her son about wanting to kill the ground squirrel. He said:

> *"Mom, that wasn't a real ground squirrel tunnel. The ground squirrel was in disguise. It was the hole all the bad guys came to our planet through. The adults just couldn't see it."*

Wow! That was the most profound and extraordinary dialogue between a mom and her five-year-old son. The best part is that when this mom voiced her concern (that others also had), the guide and the parents were able to create a dialogue that brought awareness and compassion with how to communicate with the children more consciously, and this strengthened the participants in the nature class even more. Not only did everyone feel more empowered by this experience but this mom's child was able to have his voice and feel heard from the community.

When we, as parents and caregivers, can move beyond our own fears and choose to merely ask our children what they are doing (in a gentle and inquisitive manner) vs. trying to control the situation and assume what they are doing is "bad" or harmful, it is then that we can come from an approach that nurtures our children's creativity and fosters connection. When we choose this approach, magic can happen!

As Albert Einstein once said:

> *"Imagination is more important than knowledge. Knowledge is limited. Imagination encircles the world."*

What is Permissive Parenting?

Permissive parenting and authoritarian parenting are two sides of the same coin because both are reactionary and don't place connection as a priority between parent and child. Permissive parenting can be considered another form of unconscious parenting because it places upon the child the responsibility for the emotional health of the parent. Connection becomes lost in the abyss of parental wounds which can unconsciously overshadow the relationship.

So where authoritarian parenting is about power over, permissive parenting is misappropriated power that shifts the focus on the parent rather than the child. Both philosophies are dysfunctional and do not work in creating connection.

So as to develop healthy emotions where kids feel safe and supported, they sometimes need healthy boundaries. I will be discussing this in more depth in Chapter Nine.

There is one more thing of value to share. It isn't so much about being controlled coercively, but it does create disconnection. And it is, surprisingly, the infamous saying "Good job!" I know what you're thinking. How can praise be a bad thing?

Ruth Beaglehole, founder of Echo Parenting and Education, promotes celebration over praise. She exclaimed during an FLV workshop:

"We have an epidemic with the word "Good." For instance, good job, good boy, good girl, good sitting, good eating, good climbing up the stairs, etc. What we're doing is making our children become addicted to intrinsic rewards. They become addicted to that praise. Instead of rewards, move towards a celebration through an observation. "You climbed up the stairs." Try to imagine what the experience means for the child rather than taking it away and making it through us, through our filter. And when we say "good job" what we're really saying is "I like that" and it becomes conditional parenting. If you do what I like, I praise you. If you don't do what I like, there could be silence or things taken away."

So, if you really think about it, constantly using praise causes our children to look outside of themselves for approval; approval from their parents, their teachers and other authoritative figures vs. wanting to do things for themselves, for their own approval, for the sake of making themselves feel good and content within their own choices, creative space, and feelings. And it really shouldn't be about making us proud of them and whether or not a privilege will be taken away (or worse yet, our love taken away), it should be about our children feeling proud of themselves, which can actually motivate them to want to do whatever the action was from a place of choice vs. force or fear of something being withdrawn.

Solution: What can you say or do instead of saying 'good job'? There are several ways to show your child that you are aware of their accomplishments:

- ***Show Appreciation:*** When you are appreciative, it far outweighs what any praise can do for your child and the connection between the two of you. So by saying "thank you" it is truly more effective than saying "good job." For instance, *"Thank you for cleaning up your toys. It makes it easier for all of us to walk in the room."* Or *"Thank you for helping me cook. I appreciate all the love you put in the food."*

- **_Be an Observer:_** By being observant, it actually shows that you are paying attention to what they are doing, rather than the repetitive and automatic response merely through praise. In reality, our attention is all our children want, anyways. In this example, you could say, *"You colored the picture with so many pretty colors."* This gives room for your child, if they feel the need, to talk about the picture through their own imagination. This is one key example that I'd also like to point out. It is also important to give our children a chance to share about what they did (in this case, what the child drew) vs. we adults putting forth our own thoughts and feelings about what was drawn.

  Other examples would be: *"You've been working hard on the math problems."* Or *"You slid down the slide all by yourself!"* This allows the focus to be on the action (in a non-judgmental way) vs. the result.

- **_Be Inquisitive:_** By asking questions, you are opening up an opportunity for your child to share more about their thoughts and feelings and come from a place within his creativity. For instance, *"You climbed all the way up the hill. How did that make you feel?"* This shows that you were being observant (as mentioned in the last example); and when you are asking how your child feels, it allows an opportunity for the child to express how he is feeling about it as opposed to how it is making you feel. Again, as pointed out in #2, it helps to make it more about our children vs. making it about us.

  Another example of gently leading with a question would be: *"How many steps did you take to walk up the hill?"* Or *"Why did you choose to color the sky green?"* Again, by asking questions, it gives your child a chance to describe what stemmed from his/her creative mind.

- **_Celebrate:_** Celebrating your child's achievements and goals is very different from saying 'good job.' An example where you are celebrating your child with achieving a task would be, *"Wow!*

You did it!" There are no judgments of whether it was good or bad. You are simply stating a fact that the task was done.

- **<u>Encourage Compassion:</u>** Instead of saying, *"Good job for being loving to your sister,"* or, *"I like how you shared your toy,"* mention how your child's actions are being reciprocated by the other person. This could be: *"Look at Cindy's smile. She looks happy that you are sharing the ball with her."* And the same goes for when it's a negative experience. Instead of making your child feel bad and/or "wrong," you could say, *"Do you see Bobby's body language? It looks like he is feeling uncomfortable with how you are holding him."* Taking the emphasis away from how your child's actions are making you feel (which is the core of what praising does) and gently guiding your child to see how his/her actions are making someone else feel is a better way for him/her to become more aware about being compassionate and understanding.

Beyond the time-outs, bribes, and good job's, there are other methods that parents use that are just as disheartening and manipulative. They only succeed in getting the children to do what the parents want them to do and have very little to do with the child's actual needs.

The following are some examples of disconnect and solutions that can help to strengthen the bond between the child and the adult:

Example 1: *"Stop throwing things or else!"*

Solution 1: *"I'm noticing that you're throwing things in the living room. Do you just feel like throwing? Let's go outside and find toys that are okay to throw."*

Example 2: *"Say Thank You!"* or *"What Do You Say?"*

Solution 2: Instead of forcing your child to say thank you or please (which can embarrass them and produce an insincere response), a good way to have him/her learn how to say "thank you" or "please" is by modeling it. If someone gives your child a gift, you can say "thank you" if your little one doesn't say it yet. The more you are saying it, the more your child will catch on.

Example 3: *"Share your toys."*

Solution 3A: Forcing your child to share when they are not ready can create distress and disconnection, especially when the parent grabs the toy out of their child's hand to give to another child.

When we stop persuading children to share and actually allow them the opportunity to decide on their own what they want to share, children eventually become aware of others' feelings and the benefits of generosity.

Again, here is where modeling can be a great tool to show children about thoughtfulness and respecting the space of others. I read somewhere that when planning a play date for your child's friends at your home, having a basket of your own toys is a great idea, if your child is not ready to share his/her toys. By sharing your basket of toys, you are modeling the concept of sharing to all the children present.

When the need to have a toy is so immense and urgent for a child, this is a red flag opportunity for the adult to become an observational parent by focusing on the feelings that the child is displaying vs. what the child is "doing." When we are able to remember to become an observational and questionable parent vs. a demanding parent, children can learn to genuinely and freely share from the heart.

Also, if it is a special toy that the child recently received, you can ask if he/she is ready to share it and if the answer is "No" then suggesting to put it somewhere hidden or leave it in the car for the time being is a great way for your child to feel heard and an opportunity to ask your child once the toy is hidden what toys they *are* willing to share.

For example:

"I see that Amy would really like a turn playing with the dump truck. Tommy, are you open to letting her play with it?" If Tommy is not ready, then ask if he will be ready in a couple of minutes. If he says yes, then it allows for more ease for Amy, who is waiting. In the meanwhile, let Amy know that Tommy will be ready in a couple of minutes and see if she is open to playing with something else while waiting.

Now what if Tommy says "No" and isn't ready? If he says "No," the technique listed in solution 3B below is a great approach.

> Solution 3B: "I'll Be With You While You Wait" is a great technique from Hand-in-Hand Parenting's founder, Patty Wipfler. This method utilizes something called StayListening, or a somewhat similar version of this that I like to call, Time In which I will discuss in more detail in Chapter Six. The concept is to be with your child, while empathetically helping them to move through their big feelings about not being able to have the toy or their turn with playing a game.

I wanted to share a story with you on how, when you actually take the time to connect, it is much more effective than bribes, coercion, and punishments.

While my son was playing with his friends in his homeschooling nature class, he fell down and scraped his chest. Now, my son had a hard time with wanting me to help him whenever he got hurt. Rarely did he want me to put ointment, let alone a band aid, on his boo-boos. Only after some time and some convincing (with the help of his friends who caught on quickly and allowed me to put the ointment on previous cuts they had on their bodies) was he willing to let me help him.

That night during bath time, I wanted to take the band aid off to clean it up, so that after the bath, I could apply coconut oil on it and put a fresh band aid. Since there were no other kids around to model how re-dressing the boo-boo can help it to heal, this didn't go over very well with him. For about twenty minutes, all I could do was connect with him and let him know that he was safe with me and daddy. At the end, he still wasn't going for it. I didn't try to bribe him with ice cream or a new toy in order to make him do what I wanted him to do. Nor did I force him to do it, either. I just allowed things to be for the moment.

In the meantime, his daddy continued to bathe him. Gratefully while he was soaping him down, the band aid started falling off on its own. When my son's dad noticed this, he asked our son if he would like daddy to help take the rest of it off or if he would like to take it off himself. Our son, wanting to be brave, did it himself.

Because we took the time to connect with our son and let him know that he was safe with us and just allowed things to take its course, he felt safe enough to remove the band aid on his own. Consequently, what could've been a power struggle and big emotions if his daddy and I had chosen to bribe, coerce or punish him, ended up instead being an easeful rest of the night, where my son felt empowered with his choices!

Too often in life, as parents, we try to fix things right away so that our children either get over the pain quickly or we get what we need done quickly. We live in such a fast-paced world—with all the fast food, fast technology, fast parenting techniques that we forget to slow down and connect with our children (and just as importantly, with ourselves)!

I've always thought of 'quick-fix parenting' as a mask. Just like medications are a mask to illnesses and diseases and don't really get to the root of the issue. They may relieve the symptoms for the time being, but at what cost to the rest of our well-being? The same goes for the 'quick-fix parenting' philosophy–at what cost to the quality of your relationship with your child?

Parenting through connection may seem like it takes longer; but, when you look at the overall picture, it takes just as much time to connect with your child and find strategies that elevate towards empathy, trust, and loving cooperation, as it would if you were to try and find ways to repair the damage that tend to usually follow the use of bribes, coercion, and punishments.

So the next time you feel the urge to make your child do something out of coercion/fear or perhaps just to get them to comply, ask yourself if what you are going to do or say will create connection or disconnection.

Following is a great example of how a parent can reconnect after disconnection with a tool that I learned from Pam Leo's book "Rewind, Repair, and Replay."

A mom, deep in focus, is working in her home office. Her teenage daughter comes into the room and asks if her mom can help her with homework. The mom gets upset and says *"Not now. Can't you see I'm busy? You're always bugging me at the wrong time!"* The daughter's feelings are hurt as she begins to feel that she can no longer trust in her mom to support her when she needs help. The mom soon realizes that she has taken out her own frustrations on her daughter. Before her daughter leaves the room, she gently stops her daughter to "Rewind, Repair, and Replay." The mom rewinds by acknowledging that she has said and done something hurtful. She then repairs by apologizing for taking out her frustrations on her daughter. She further admits that she was dealing with a hot issue for work and that it's overwhelming her, but that it's no excuse to treat her poorly. Then she continues to repair by letting her daughter know that she didn't deserve to be treated that way. Finally, she replays by lovingly responding and letting her daughter know that she can help her in about 15 minutes, once she is done troubleshooting.

By using this method, it gave space for the mom to become aware of her own "stuff" (also allowing the daughter to know that her mom is human and can be vulnerable too), while reassuring the daughter that she can once again trust in her mom's support.

Parents' Misunderstood Perception About "Tantrums"

Tantrums, otherwise known in better terms, "Big Feelings" or "Flooded Feelings" is commonly portrayed by parents as the child being manipulative. But this couldn't be further from the truth.

Have you ever heard the phrase by Dan Millman (author of *The Way of the Peaceful Warrior*), *"The ones who are hardest to love are usually the ones who need it the most"*? Well, when a child is right smack in the middle of flooded feelings, let's say at the grocery store, most parents end up feeling embarrassed and upset. Unfortunately, this is when most parents disconnect. But as mentioned above, children cannot help but feel their feelings. Especially in those moments of frustration and upset, what children need most is connection. They need our empathy, acknowledgment, and support. And as challenging and hard as it may seem, this is the exact time when they need our love.

So let's rehash on what was discussed in this chapter. We talked about the negative effects of authoritarian and permissive parenting, showed examples that create separation and provided solutions to help resolve the disconnect.

In the upcoming chapter, I will go over the most important topic in this book. It is the opposite of isolation. It is what every human being, what every living species identifies with and cannot live without for long periods of time and that term is called...well, I guess you're just going to have to turn the page to find out.

Chapter Four:
What Is the Key to Creating Quality Relationships in Your Family?

"Nothing ever exists entirely alone; everything is in relation to everything else."
~ Buddha

Connection...connection...connection! I'm sure by now you have guessed what the key element is to creating quality relationships.

Larry Benet, known as "The Connector to Billionaires and Millionaires," once pointed out that in order to have a highly successful business, it is the quality of your relationships that truly counts. And the key to creating quality relationships is through your connections. I don't think he was just talking about the old adage of 'who you know' in the business, either.

I believe his message goes deeper than that. It's not just about rubbing elbows with the elite or lying on a casting couch to get to where you want to go in life. He's talking about the same type of connection for which I'm an advocate - which gives one a real sense of bonding that not only brings you closer to each other but uplifts each other to be who you truly are in order to succeed in life.

When I heard Larry speak about connection at a writer's conference, the very topic that I'm so passionate about, my ears perked up. I could literally feel the inspiration rushing through my veins like electricity does to a circuit board brought to life. It was refreshing to hear someone of his stature speak his truth in a way that aligned so much to the message I believe in. Because it's not just the quality of our relationships in the business world that is important, it is also in the quality of how we relate to our children.

Sometimes finding ways to connect with our children in today's fast-paced world, with so much to do and so little time, can be challenging.

Especially if we are hoping to raise confident, compassionate, as well as emotionally and socially healthy children.

Jeff Olson, an entrepreneur in relationship marketing and author of The Slight Edge, discusses how doing the little things over and over again can create a compound effect with your business. Jeff's main passion is helping others to achieve greatness in their lives through personal development.

Okay, I'm sure by now you must be thinking, *"What do these two businessmen have to do with parenting?"*

Well, we all know that parenting is the toughest job we will ever have. Larry Benet and Jeff Olson (who are parents themselves) know all too well how important it is to connect and do the little things that over time will create success in their businesses. So in parenting, it is exactly the same! When we do the little things continuously, develop personal growth through getting our own needs met, as well as foster connection with our children, spouses and co-parents unconditionally (if one is present), the compound effect of a successful, harmonious, and respectful environment within the home can be achieved.

Entrepreneurs are constantly thinking outside the box. They tend to not abide by the same rules as a person who works for a boss at a nine-to-five job. The seven key points I am about to share with you in this book also tend to not follow the same rules or style of either authoritarian or permissive parenting. So just as an entrepreneur thinks beyond the "norm," so, too, will the parenting philosophy within these pages, which will share tools on how you can connect with your children.

Steeped within these pages, I will be diving into the depths of connection and just how deeply akin we truly are to one another and to the planet.

We will explore:

- Why touch is so important

- Attachment parenting and its benefits

- Connection in nature

- Nutrition and how it relates to behavior

This chapter is probably one of the most important chapters in this book. Just like honeybees are fundamental when it comes to pollination and continuing the cycle of our eco-system on earth, so is connection when it comes to creating a relationship with others that fosters confidence, compassion, and cooperation.

There are many statistics out there that show the difference in adults who are raised with unconditional love, connection and empathy vs. adults who were brought up in a coercive and distressful environment.

In terms of survival, are connection and the sensation of touch even really that necessary? The answer is yes! When an infant is born, in order to stimulate the production of growth hormone and the immune system, he/she needs physical affection. Without it, the body will start to shut down and can actually die from lack of touch. Statistics have shown that 99% of babies in orphanages in the United States died before they were seven months old. Although it was reported approximately a hundred years ago, it is still up to this day considered a severe form of malnutrition called marasmus, which is caused from the deprivation of skin-to-skin contact. The good news is this condition can be reversed by simply surrounding the infant with nurturing affection.

This is why attachment parenting plays a vital role in bridging the gap between connection and disconnection. If you think about it, your little one has been attached to you for nine months inside the womb, so it would only make sense that the baby would need to feel your touch in order to feel soothed and to develop healthily outside of the womb.

So what is attachment parenting, exactly? Dr. William Sears, a highly respected and well-known pediatrician, coined the term attachment parenting (AP) as a style in which nurturing connection is the main focus. Such practices as baby bonding, baby wearing, breastfeeding, and co-sleeping are a few of the techniques that are believed to help raise secure, independent and empathetic children into adults.

Throughout my pregnancy, I did extensive research on this particular topic (not to mention on cloth diapering, elimination communication and non-toxic/organic living).

In witnessing my dear friend's children, whose ages range from 5 years old to 23, I have had the wonderful chance to see first-hand how AP (along with other conscious parenting methods) has positively influenced her adult children (as well as the younger ones) and her whole family dynamic. It is inspiring to watch how her whole family connects and communicates with one another and others around them so genuinely.

Going back to connection, there is a whole spectrum of concepts related to how we, as a species on Planet Earth, connect to one another. And the connection doesn't stop there with us humans and creatures. All of life is interconnected. And this, too, can be best demonstrated in nature. I find it quite fascinating that when there is a poisonous plant, such as poison oak in the woods, that not too far down the path is the antidote.

Years ago, humans were so much more connected to nature and had a much more tranquil relationship with it. There was a time when we used plants to heal our ailments and relied on the stars and the sun as our compass and time-teller. Our source of food was pure and free of chemicals and slow cooking was the best way to receive healthy nutrition. Nowadays, people are addicted to the quick fix with using pharmaceutical drugs that tend to mask the illness or pain but don't get to the root of the issue. It is a time when our "smart cars" or "smart phones" navigate us and fast food and fast cooking (via a microwave or a can) continues to be the staple for many American meals.

It has been known that nature can promote healing and can relieve stress. The more we allow ourselves, for instance, to enjoy how it feels to have our bare toes touching the many blades of newly cut grass or to go for a nice hike in the mountains, the more we are able to tap into a more easeful and aware state of being. Studies show that when you come back to nature and immerse yourself in its healing energy, this creates even more connection to yourself and to others.

When it comes to our food supply, this poses a big concern, as the foods we eat are not as natural as they used to be. Could what we are feeding our children and ourselves be affecting our behavior? The answer is a definite yes! We are in a day and age where there are more allergies and sensitivities to foods than ever before. If you really think about it, when you were growing up, there weren't as many allergies going around. I rarely recall our parents having to find different food options for their children's friends at birthday parties. Nor was there much to offer in allergen-free food choices back then; perhaps it was because sensitivities to foods weren't as frequent. Nowadays, allergies are an epidemic that parents are getting attuned to. At least within the community of families I know, we do our best to offer gluten-free, peanut-free, and dairy-free options. And there are more of these options in restaurants, too. But as thankful as I am to have these options for my family, one has to wonder why there are so many more options and allergies considered as commonplace in this day and age?

This brings me back to my family's experience when we first discovered our son's food sensitivities. When my son was about seven months old, I started noticing salmon-colored bleeding in his cloth diapers. For a whole month, the doctors couldn't figure out what was causing this discoloring. All the grueling blood tests, stool tests, and urine tests that my son had to endure came up negative. It wasn't until my son's dad and I went to a holistic doctor (Dr. Timothy R. Campbell, D.C.) that we discovered that our son was sensitive to wheat/gluten and dairy through my breast milk.

Not all parents are able to discover sensitivities in their infant's diet (or in this case, my own diet that was affecting my son through my breast milk). The food sensitivities were affecting my son on a physical level, but there are many children who are affected on a behavioral level, too. With the amount of sugars, preservatives, artificial flavors, food dyes, GMO's, and crops infested with pesticides that are frequently found in our food supply, it comes as no surprise. And did you know that wheat is actually being sprayed with Round-Up 10 days before being harvested because it increases the yield by 30%? This means we end up having residue of Round-Up in our foods which can run havoc on our bodies' internal system of organs.

Behavioral issues such as ADD, ADHD, Autism, and Alzheimer's are more prevalent these days. There could be many causes, but one that tends to go unlooked is the American diet. It has been reported that approximately seventeen studies showed that diet can sometimes dramatically affect one's behavior.

When it comes to emotional and physical ailments, my family has always sought out holistic practitioners to help get to the root cause of any pain or discomfort experienced. In fact, it was taking my son to see a holistic doctor that helped us solve the mystery of the discoloration in my son's diaper in the first place. This isn't to say that we don't seek out Western medicine when absolutely necessary. I just prefer researching my options when it comes to my family's health, doing preventative maintenance by eating organic, non-gmo whole foods and seeking holistic medicine and doctors first before anything else.

One of the modalities for which we are advocates is called Applied Kinesiology (AK) and NET (Neuro-Emotional Technique) - which is a fascinating and effective combined scientific system. In applied kinesiology, they consider health as a triangle. The three legs of the triangle include structure and biochemistry, as well as one's emotional state. In order to attain optimal health, all sides of the triad must be equal to one another. When an individual has less than optimal health, there is usually an imbalance in one or more of these areas of health.

So now that you've gotten an idea about what types of things can cause behavior issues, below are several tips that Dr. Campbell shared when he was a guest speaker for FLV.

The following can help as preventative maintenance for you and your child's brain and well-being. Information and statements made are for education purposes and are not intended to replace the advice of your doctor. This information does not dispense medical advice, prescribe or diagnose illness. The views and nutritional advice expressed here are not intended to be a substitute for conventional medical service. If you or your child have a severe medical condition or health concern, see your physician.

Tips for Optimal Health

- Eat a whole-food diet that consists of vegetables, fruits and other foods closest to its natural state and unprocessed. Avoid foods that have GMO's, food dyes and colors, nitrates, pesticides, gluten, sugar, artificial flavors, fast foods, as well as overly processed, microwaved foods. If you continue eating foods that are chemically infested, it can decrease the quality of your health while possibly increasing the chances of you and/or your child's behavior becoming more aggravated.

- My added input: For those who eat meat and fish, eating meat that is grass-fed and fish that is wild-caught, as well as supporting and buying from organizations that treat animals humanely is a big part of how food can affect one's health. We have all heard the saying, *"You are what you eat."*

- So here's a question to ponder on: if you are eating foods that have chemicals, are genetically modified and come from animals who have been mistreated (and are most likely sick due to the mistreatment), could it not affect your body and your mind? Now in contrast to what I just asked, another important thing to ponder on is to intuitively go with what you feel is True for you and what feels good for you to ingest, as well. I will go deeper into this concept in Chapter Ten.

- If someone in your family tends to get sick often, he/she may have issues with their gut. The immune system is usually 60% in the digestive tract, so having a good quality probiotic is a must!

- Drink at least eight glasses of water daily! Dehydration is the number one reason why people come into Dr. Campbell's office. If you're dehydrated, you're not polar to begin with. We are made up of about 80% water. Ideally if you're urinating four times a day, you're losing about eight ounces each time. So 8 x 4 = 32. So you're losing about a quart of water through urination. And with the moisture that is released when breathing, that would be another quart. If you do any type of exercise and are perspiring, there's another 1/2 to one quart. So we are about three quarts down with water each day. As they age, people start losing height on their vertebrae. The disks in the vertebrae are made up of about 70% water. People who are not drinking enough water might discover they have dehydrated disks by the time they reach their 50's and 60's; at that point, it is pretty tough to rehydrate them. So again, drink lots of water!

- Sugar is the second top reason that people go to see Dr. Campbell. People are taking in too much processed sugar. Even Agave is now considered comparable to white sugar. So when it comes to ADD & ADHD, sugar can increase hyperactivity. To neutralize adults and kids, who have been diagnosed with ADD & ADHD, they should take B-Complex, use good quality oils, stay hydrated and change their diet.

- Avoid Agave, white sugar and Aspartame (otherwise known as amino sweetener)! Yes, even agave is considered an unhealthy sugar! Both agave and white sugar get processed through an acid wash, which then turns it white. Aspartame breaks down into formic acid and formaldehyde. Formic acid has the same effect as a bite from an ant or a bee sting, while formaldehyde is the same stuff used to embalm the deceased! Ew...not a mixture I prefer putting into my body!

- Some good sugars to use are dark sugar cane, Stevia, and Xylitol. On a side note, just like chocolate, it is advisable to keep Xylitol away from dogs.

- Cook with organic coconut oil, organic peanut oil or organic grape seed oil. These three options can handle heat. AVOID soy oil and canola oil, since they are inflammatory and toxic. Do NOT cook with olive oil. It doesn't do well with heat. It breaks down and becomes carcinogenic and causes more pollution and toxins within the body.

- Coconut oil is good to help with the digestive tract, because lauric acid is an active component in it. Just like mother's milk, lauric acid helps the immune system.

- Onions and garlic are good for your liver. They have a lot of sulfur in them. It helps to kill parasites, bacteria and viruses. But if you do take garlic pills, you have to make sure they are NOT odorless because the odorless supplements don't work as well.

- Avoid taking too many painkillers. If you take painkillers repeatedly, they can start to shut down your nervous system. To help with pain, try Turmeric and White Willow [or other holistic medicine that can create more balance between Western and Eastern medicine].

- If you have TMJ (grinding of the teeth), you may want to get a plate guard (called a warming fit) to wear at night. Use the mouth guard in the bottom jaw, because, in the upper jaw, the mouth guard would restrict normal cranial motion. As an interesting side note, a lot of C-section babies have cranium issues because cranium bones don't compress during a C-section birth.

- Kangen water is popularly known to help people get into an alkaline type state. Stomach enzymes are usually at a 2-4 pH, which allows the food to digest and also kill bacteria, parasites, and viruses. Often, when medical establishments prescribe someone to take drugs for their ailments, it changes the gut. Although not ideal (because it only helps the symptom but not the cause), if you were to take antacids like Maalox, Pepto Bismol, Tums or Predaset, it will change your gut into an alkaline state. But the reason why you may experience heartburn in the first place is because the pyloric valve at the end of the stomach needs to sense the Ph at 2-4, so that the food bolus can go into the small intestine for assimilation. Alcohol gets broken down into formaldehyde if there isn't enough "b" complex in the system for the complete breakdown.

- As we get older, after 35 years or so, we start to produce less and less HCL in the stomach, which in turn can cause the acid reflux to act like a simmering pot. When this happens, it can overflow and go into the esophagus, which could cause esophagus erosion. To avoid this from happening (or to help the situation), you need to raise the hydrochloric acid and then get the acids in your stomach down by changing your diet, as well as taking Zinc and a B complex.

So when treating health issues, as the saying goes, "treat the root cause, not the symptoms" because although the symptoms might seem apparent, we don't want to confuse them with the cause.

In some cases, there can be a psychological reversal. So let's just say if someone is dealing with depression, it could be caused by a sugar imbalance which prohibits the neurotransmitters from getting in and doing what they're supposed to do. This could give us a clue to why Parkinson's, ADD/ADHD, dementia, and other diseases are rampant. So to help prevent these diseases, it is always a good idea to seek professional advice from a holistic specialist who can look at the overall triad of your family's health and not just one or two components of it. It truly is about preventative maintenance and although buying organic, nonGMO, pasture-raised, and grass-fed foods and products may see like it costs more, even as a single mom, I truly see the benefit in supporting a vibrant and healthy immune system for my family. I would rather spend the money now with preventative maintenance than to spend thousands of dollars with hospital bills and a weakened immune system when I'm older due to not taking care of this vehicle of mine. Just like you would want to maintain your car with the highest grade products so that your car runs at its peak performance, wouldn't you want the same for your own body, as well? Just something to ponder on.

So now that we've gone over a wide range of how everything is interconnected, I wanted to share two stories about connection, behavior, and bullying. A great example of how connection can create a strong parent/child bond is a story that one of the Family Love Village mamas shared with me.

My friend, Sonia Wike (a Homeschool Educational Specialist), and her then two-year old daughter wanted to make homemade play dough. So they went to the store to get the ingredients. One of the main ingredients is flour; and, of course, what does the two-year old discover while walking down the aisle to get the flour? Rows and rows of cookies, doughnuts, and tons of sweets wrapped in cartoon characters such as Blues Clues and Dora the Explorer – you know, the deceptive marketing strategies that these companies do to reel our children in?!

Of course, the little girl got excited and said, *"Ooh! I want this one and this one and this one,"* as she grabbed for the boxes. The mom, instead of saying, *"No you can't have that!"* got down to her daughter's level to make eye contact and then said, *"You know, I get that you think these boxes look really fun because of all the cartoon characters. And that these packages look really pretty and shiny and colorful on the outside, but on the inside it's really full of sugar and icky stuff that's really not healthy for your body."*

The next thing that happened shocked my friend. Her two-year old looked at the boxes, thought about it and put them back. Her two-year old! Then the same thing happened when they were waiting in line to pay for their items and her daughter saw candy and chocolate on the rack. You know, the rack that is just screaming at kids, *"Pick me!"* so that they can beg their parents to buy the junk food right before paying at the register. My friend gently reminded her daughter about what she had mentioned earlier and they were able to leave the grocery store to enjoy the rest of their day.

Stories like this and my own experiences of connection with my son continue to inspire me and ignite such passion in wanting to share in the possibilities of finding ways to partner with our children consciously vs. being authoritarian and bullying (which makes you wonder where children's bullying stems from, right?)

Now it may not always pan out the way it did for my friend but the fact that she took the time to explain why it wouldn't be a good idea to have the sweets vs. just saying *"Because I said so,"* really made such the difference in their experience for that moment and for the rest of their day, as a matter of fact.

Speaking of bullying, here's another story that I'd like to share that is an example of how using 'quick-fix parenting' tactics creates disconnection.

I remember witnessing something quite interesting when I took my son to the park. There was a man with his son (who was about seven years old at the time) sitting at a park bench table. The dad was trying to help his son with his homework – well, more like getting frustrated with his son for not understanding his homework. The son was skipping some of the questions and doing the questions that he did understand. All of a sudden, his dad gets up and says that they're done doing homework at the park and he has to do the rest when he gets home. Because he felt his son wasn't listening to him, the dad wanted to punish him by saying that they had to leave the park.

His son was obviously upset with this news and started doing the other questions to try and prove to his dad that he could do the rest of the math problems. Instead of partnering with his son and finding a way to help him get through his homework, the dad did probably the only thing he knew how (which most parents tend to do when they're frustrated and overwhelmed). He gave him an ultimatum that if he didn't follow through, there would be consequences. In this case, he threatened to leave him.

Even with his son trying to show him that he could do the homework, possibly the dad felt like he now had to somehow prove to his son that he had to go through with the threat and show him that there are repercussions for not listening to him. So he started walking towards the car and warned him that he was leaving. Unfortunately this led to his son crying out loud and heartbroken, saying something to the effect of, *"I can do better. Please don't leave me!"* His dad came back (probably embarrassed) and said something similar to the effect of, "All right! Then listen to me and finish the rest of your homework."

Most likely the reward for the son to finish his homework was to play on the playground afterwards. During this entire time, my son and I were playing underneath a bridge on the sand. After the boy was done with his homework, he came up and asked if he could play with us. For about five to ten minutes, he played happily with us and then soon his friends, who were around his age, arrived at the park.

And here is where it gets interesting. When he was playing with his other friends, I noticed that he started becoming a bully with them; telling them what to do and making them play the way he wanted them to play; and if they didn't comply, then they couldn't play with his toys. Sound familiar?

The little boy was basically acting out what his dad was doing to him, only now towards his friends. And because he and his dad weren't able to reconnect in a loving way, he ended up letting out his feelings towards his friends, the only way he knew how (the way that his dad was modeling it to him).

So if you still wonder if the *"I'm leaving you if you're not ready"* tactic works, sure it can. And sure, they may listen to you, get ready in a jiffy and head out the door; but, it's only because they truly fear that you will leave them behind. This quick-fix strategy only creates disconnection and makes your child scared that you would actually leave them at home or at the mall, or in this case, the park.

As mentioned earlier, living in today's society, parents tend to find the "quick fix," fast food, fast solution; but more often than not, in the long run, this creates disconnected, unhealthy adults who live in a disconnected and unhealthy world.

Carmine Leo, founder of www.lifecoaching.com and an expert in emotional intelligence, has been a huge influence on my path with parenting through connection. He and Pam Leo used to facilitate Connection Parenting workshops together, so he is very familiar with the philosophy that Pam has written about in her book. Through Carmine's mentoring with my first Connection Parenting workshop, the confidence he instilled in me is how Family Love Village came to be.

In a recent interview I conducted with him, he voiced the most profound message that I'd like to share:

> *"There needs to be a recognition of Gaia. This is a planetary organism, the species of all life, the atmosphere and chemistry, the oceans and land, and the living and nonliving parts. This is a self-regulating organism - perhaps a level of consciousness of the bacteria. But it's got its own metabolism and homeostasis just like you do in your body. Gaia in the pure science, regulates the chemistry in the oceans and the atmosphere in ways that are prosperous for life. This civilization has been damaging that beyond telling. So now Gaia is waking up and she is really catching a fever and I tell you what. She'll shake us off like a bad case of fleas unless we wake up and get with the program and live in sustainable ways again; connected to the earth!*
>
> *The first place that we connect to the earth is to connect to each other. And we do that within our family and how we raise our children that can open the door to the connection, the empathy and the conscience. [Connection gives us] the ability to look at another being, whether it has fur, scales, feathers or fins and recognize that this life is profoundly connected to our own. We've lost that connection and*

connection parenting and the work that you are doing through Family Love Village is re-establishing that connection and is opening the way again to reconnect to the planetary life."

This statement left me speechless, and although he couldn't see me, I was shaking my head rigorously in complete agreement with every word Carmine uttered. I was like a child, fully engaged and clinging onto every syllable, every word, every sentence, as if he were reading the most fascinating book to me.

So in order to live in harmony with the planet, as Carmine so wonderfully expressed, we must first begin with our children and ourselves.

Just as I mentioned about Jeff Olson earlier, when we do the little things consistently over time, the compound effect in the long run can create a huge impact in our lives. The same holds true when we do the little things to strengthen the bond in our family – the results of connection to ourselves, to our children, to one another, and to the planet will spread like wildfire.

The baby steps could be anywhere from taking time to breathe when you're feeling frustrated, reading ten pages a day of a personal development book (a tip that Jeff Olson suggests in his book, *The Slight Edge*), spending ten minutes connecting with your kids and/or spouse/loved one, feeding your body with nutritious whole foods or perhaps sinking your bare feet into the sand while basking in the sun.

To summarize, everything is connected and how we connect to everything is central to how we, as parents, can foster confidence, compassion, and cooperation in our children. Anywhere from conception to birth to attachment parenting to how we fuel our own bodies...these are all essential elements in how we decide to raise our children, consciously. And not just our children but how we choose to raise one another, how we choose to raise Mother Earth and all creatures and living things on the planet, as well as how we are raising and loving ourselves. We do have a choice and the more we become aware of our choices – whether to buy into big corporations or to support local, sustainable companies; whether to continue buying into the industrial farming industry or supporting more humanely-raised farming practices, whether we choose to buy into over-consumption or choosing not to use single use items, such as plastic straws and other plastic-ware; whether to choose harsh chemically-infested products or more eco-friendly and biodegradable products. We do have a choice – it is just a matter of becoming aware of our choices and choosing a more conscious and connected choice with raising our children, one another, our planet, and ourselves. Because, what we choose can and has been affecting our society and our world. It is time for us to become Planet Protectors, to take a stand and have our voices heard in a way that moves beyond hate and disconnection.

We have all been so deeply programmed in our society and ingrained with a "power over", that it is now time to shift our perception to a lens of empathy and create a stance of "working with". It all begins with how we are consciously raising our children, how we are consciously raising/uplifting one another, and how we are raising Mama Gaia. Because, somehow, I have a feeling that Mama Gaia will live on with or without us and the generations that follow in our footsteps. It all depends on how we are choosing to raise one another up (or not to). So it is up to us to come together as a conscious community and collectively find ways to stand together; not against each other. From the two-legged to the four-legged to the scaled, and the winged; to the land, to the oceans, to the air – all of it is an interwoven symbiosis of connection.

To summarize, let's review the key to creating quality relationships in your family. So now that we have a better understanding of how everything is intertwined, even down to what we put into our bodies, that can affect how we connect to life, what does it really mean to raise our children up consciously? Up next, we will go over what it means to be a conscious parent in today's society. So make sure to turn the page to learn more.

Chapter Five:
What is Conscious Parenting?

"No problem can be solved from the same level of consciousness that created it"
~ Albert Einstein

As parents, we do our best with what we know, but what if what we don't know is really the issue at hand? What if our ignorance to wanting to learn another philosophy to parenting is getting in the way of our children thriving, including the relationship with our children? And if there is another way, what are the tools we can use to create a mutually respectful way to communicate with one another?

The term "conscious parenting," gratefully, has started to spring up more often these days in conversations between like-minded and curious parents, with books and DVDs, as well as organizations that provide training and support through online and in-person classes. Parents and caregivers are becoming more aware of not just wanting to provide their children with their basic needs, but their emotional and spiritual needs, as well. And when I speak of "spiritual," I'm talking about the essence of a child's pure spirit, his/her pure innocence.

Too often I hear a parent yelling at their child because the parent is embarrassed that their son is having big feelings (a.k.a. tantrums) in the store, or I witness a grandparent lightly spanking her granddaughter for not "behaving" the way they want them to behave. The majority of authoritative figures in our society only know what they know, and, in most cases, feel that what they are doing is at least not as bad as they had it when they were younger. Which might sadly be the truth, but it still doesn't mean that it won't dim the light within these children and cause potential emotional and spiritual damage in one form or another.

Have you ever heard of the old saying "ignorance is bliss"? It is based on the concept that what you don't know can't hurt you. But the truth is, it's hurting your child, which can ultimately hurt you and the relationship you have or don't have with them. So how do we move away from ignorance? The first step is to make a cognizant choice to want to learn ways in becoming a conscious parent.

In this chapter, we will go over:

- What it means to be a conscious parent

- Ways to become more aware with your children

So what does it really mean to consciously parent your children? To some, it could mean being aware of your natural and holistic wellness choices for your family. To others, it could mean doing your best to eat organic, grass-fed and non-processed foods. For still others, it's about living a non-toxic lifestyle and being eco-friendly. It could mean creating a parent/child bond that instills partnership in "power with" instead of "power over"… for several others, it is striving to model a healthy and loving relationship between the parents. It is nurturing a more simplistic lifestyle with less media access, less stuff, and more nature and child-led play. It is about attachment parenting, breastfeeding and co-sleeping, seeking support when you're not getting your own needs met or perhaps finding a community that resonates with your parenting philosophies…and for many, perhaps it's about actually taking that first step in making the choice to become a conscious parent!

For my family, including my organization, Family Love Village (FLV), it can be all of the above. Yet, it is wherever you are at on your parenting path and knowing that it is okay – that we're all striving to model the best that we can so that our children can thrive! Conscious parenting is not about the destination. It is about the journey and the commitment to continuously travel upwards on that journey. And if we are to travel upward then what Albert Einstein quoted above is completely true.

Sadly, as you have read in the previous chapters, other parenting methods usually depend on tools that aren't so conscious. My family and a lot of FLVillage members prefer navigating with tools and resources through several of our programs that help educate us and our children towards becoming advocates in holistic wellness and sustainable promoters for our planet. As well, we believe in a more gently guided approach that not only creates connection, but allows children to fully access their compassionate intelligence along with the innate ability to unconditionally love and be loved. If you think about it, that is really all that anyone ever wants to feel – to be loved and accepted by others. So why not BE the shift in role modeling that guides our children with experiencing conscious living, where they can pay it forward for generations to come?

Conscious parenting also entails nonviolence, and it's not only about the physicality of nonviolence, either. It means to fully respect the life force of another human being, animal and/or plant life. At birth, most people love their children deeply. Love is essential to infant brain development and determines whether or not a child will thrive later in life. Yet, this love can get compromised by a lot of things, such as stress, fear, finances, unresolved problems or a parent's own unresolved childhood trauma.

This is where Nonviolent Communication, developed by Marshall Rosenberg (founder of NVC) and later acquired by Ruth Beaglehole (founder of Echo Parenting and Education), can help. NVC can delete blame, shame, judgment, manipulation, and domination (including praise and rewards). It helps the parent to look past the behavior of anger, anxiety and withdrawal in order to know that it is usually the emptied love cup that is threatening the parent/child connection. It not only gives parents tools to build a foundation of family values that embrace warmth, compassion and loving boundaries, it also helps to break the vicious cycle of violent thoughts, feelings ,and/or actions around childhood trauma that can get projected onto their children.

When it comes to conscious parenting, I strongly believe that creating conscious connection is vital within the family dynamic and I do my best to focus on the relationship vs. the behavior. So instead of focusing on my son's behavior and how to "control" his feelings, I strive to get to the root of his big feelings and partner in finding ways to release them.

I encourage my son to "let it out" and express his feelings in a healthy space to heal and self-soothe. Letting it out is very different from "crying it out." Letting it out allows him to release all of his feelings, which allows him to re-regulate himself. Most parents become uncomfortable with the bellowing tears, and the majority of the time they are trying to find ways to get their children to stop. And if you think about it, even as infants, parents and caregivers tend to "shush" the babies in an attempt to calm them down. Yet these cries are their way of communicating their unmet need. The same goes for a toddler "tantrum" or a teenager's "bad" attitude – it is a communication of an unmet need, whether physically or emotionally.

Going back to the concept of "letting it out" – whenever my son has big feelings, I am present with him and I lovingly hold the space for him to move through his feelings. Allowing a child to "cry it out" is completely different. This initiates disconnection and makes children feel unloved, insecure and distrustful of others, as I had mentioned in Chapter Two. Sure, eventually they will stop crying, but at what expense? And yes, they will stop crying, but not because their grief has been alleviated but because they soon learn that they can no longer trust and rely on the parent/caregiver to provide comfort and support. As mentioned in Chapter Four, touch is fundamental for a baby's well-being so it is important to pick up the baby to comfort her when crying.

Now not every child will want to "let it out" with their feelings. Letting their feelings out may be too scary for them. So conscious parenting also entails being observant to what works best for your child and your family dynamic.

For my family, when it comes to consciously parenting, I practice an approach that is gently guided, yet still entails setting boundaries in a loving and empathetic environment without fear-based methods and/or using praise, rewards or punishments. I'm definitely not perfect, nor do I want to be (because if I were, there would be no room to grow). And when I do slip back into old habits of recycled upbringing tactics, being conscious of that and reconnecting with my son is key.

Through continuous education and a desire to find another way to parent, a lifestyle has evolved that allows me to embrace connection, eco-friendliness, whole body-mind-spirit holistic wellness and a homeschooling approach to living. I know the "real world" is not 'out there somewhere' but instead is everywhere, particularly in what we role model at home. Most importantly, mindful parenting consists of reminding ourselves as parents and as human beings, about self-care and self-love; remembering that we matter. When we take care of our own needs, our children will observe that and over time their capacity to grow and discover ways to be conscious and centered will inspire healthy relationships with themselves and others.

There's a great quote from a mentor of mine, Amir Zoghi, who is an International leader and speaker in the area of self awareness and human potential. Zoghi says,

> *"The difference between a prison and a mind that is unconscious is that an unconscious mind may not yet realize that it's in prison."*

This rings true for parenting, as well. If we continue to go about our daily lives unaware of how we are treating our children (or just as importantly, how we are treating ourselves) in what ways would we be modeling for our children to treat others and themselves, as well? Would we then, metaphorically, be teaching our children to build their own jail cells...to become prisoners, shackled to their own limiting beliefs that when they grow up to be adults can take years of therapy to heal?

And what would it take for us to become attentive and mindful? To begin consciously choosing to create a home in which everyone feels safe and has a voice. A place where love is given and received freely without an agenda, expectation or condition. Where everyone's needs are considered valid and important and connection is the cement that binds the foundation together.

This is the path we can all choose for ourselves and for our children. It just takes putting one foot in front of the other to move in this direction. When you move your feet, the body will follow. And it doesn't mean you have to sprint to get there. It can be taken in baby steps. But the only way it can be done is if you consciously make the choice to take that first step.

Now that we have gotten a better understanding of the brain, children's development, the many levels of trauma, how we are connected to everything and what defines parenting from a consciously, heart-based space, the next several chapters we will dive into the seven principles that have been proven to work. The upcoming chapters will give more detail on tools from articles I have written, along with other tools and resources from the many mentors from whom I've learned. They have proven their weight in gold in relation to the deeper connection I now have with my son and I have witnessed them working for other families, as well.

So now it's time to take that baby step and turn the page to pull the veil from our eyes to see with a different lens that can allow a deeper connection within our homes and to build that core infrastructure that can withstand any prison.

Chapter Six:
What is the Triad of Connection?

"The wise old owl lived in an oak;
The more he saw the less he spoke;
The less he spoke the more he heard:
Why can't we all be like that bird?"
~ Edward H. Richards

When I read this quote, it really spoke to me. So many times, as parents, when trying to get our point across to our kids, we end up expelling, or what I like to call "vomiting," all our stuff onto them, vomiting our opinions, our disapproval and our disappointments. We try to lecture them in that moment and make them do what we want them to do. In all of this talking, we forget to listen.

In Chapter One, we talked about when children are in their lower brain and their limbic system is full of emotions and they are experiencing heightened cortisol levels of distress; it is difficult for children to hear what we are trying to tell them. And it doesn't even have to be our words that affect a child's ability to listen. Our own body language and how we are communicating energetically can affect them just the same.

Did you know that 95% of communication is nonverbal? The majority of our communication stems from our facial expressions, body language, gestures and our tone of voice. When speaking to our children, it is important to communicate empathetically, because it is through our modeling that they, too, will learn how to communicate towards others.

So what can we do, as parents, to get our children to listen? We must first, by example, elicit the tool of listening in order for it to be followed. Just like Edward H. Richards' quote above, we must become the owl and speak less, so we can listen to the underlying, unmet need that our children are trying to express to us through their behavior.

During my research and adventures in conscious parenting, I stumbled across an online resource called Hand in Hand Parenting. The founder, Patty Wipfler, has a couple of tools that I have found to be completely helpful on my journey.

Along with one of my own tools and two of Hand in Hand Parenting's, this is what I call the Triad of Connection. When using these three tools, the connection that arises is almost miraculous! In this chapter, you will learn:

- What the Triad of Connection is
- How the Triad of Connection works
- The benefits of using these tools to create more connection

Time In

Instead of the traditional time-outs that most adults are used to and where the child feels isolated by themselves, having Time In allows a child to offload his/her feelings while the parent/caregiver attentively listens to the child. As we know from Chapter Three, time-outs only act as a band-aid and don't work towards getting to the root of your child's behavior.

There is a beautiful quote by Cheryl Richardson that states: *"People start to heal the moment they feel heard."* This philosophy needs to replace the old saying, *"Children should be seen and not heard"* that most of us parents were raised in. It is time to get rid of recycled parenting patterns that are damaging to the relationship with our children and find ways to strengthen it.

When you take the time to be there for your child, calmly and lovingly, he will trust in you and feel safe enough to release his emotions without feeling abandoned and left to deal with his feelings on his own; he also won't feel forced to stop crying/venting and feeling. The end result when this tool is used is a child who feels heard, supported through the big feelings and more able to cooperate.

Here's what the process might look like:

You and your child just finished watching a TV show together. You explained to him 15 minutes prior to it ending that this will be the last show for the evening. He seemed to be fine with the explanation in that moment; but once you turn off the TV, you begin to notice him having flooded feelings because he is sad that the fun is over. He asks to watch just one more show and instead of getting frustrated and saying *"No, you can't"*, you acknowledge and empathize with his feelings and do Time In with him. *"I can see if it were up to you, you'd stay up later to watch another show. I get it. It's hard to stop doing something you enjoy. It's getting late though and we need to get ready for bed."* At this point, he may cooperate or possibly get even more upset. This is where you can continue having Time In and connect with him as he offloads his feelings.

Although it may seem like it takes longer to do a Time In to connect and help your child through his upset feelings, it takes just as long for him to heal from the coercion and punishments that can be much more tempting to fall back on and just as detrimental to his well-being.

Here's a great example of the Time In tool that happened with my son:

My son, who was four years old at the time, was always used to me being the one to put him to sleep. Although it is a wonderful way for us to connect while cuddling and reading books, there were nights when I needed to get things done (like when I was writing this book, for instance). So for quite some time, my son's dad would try to put him to sleep. It always started out smoothly; we would set the stage (an effective technique I will share in Chapters Eight and Nine) and let our son know that I would be in the office working and that he would be with daddy. He would be happy and excited that daddy was reading to him, but once that last page of the book was finished, he would start unraveling at the seams and end up crying for me. No amount of comforting on his dad's part would help. It never failed – our son would run out of the bedroom and come flying into the office in tears. I would then allow him to crawl into my lap to fall asleep in my arms while I was working and then bring him into the bedroom afterwards. It definitely was not ideal, but sometimes it was the only way I could get stuff done. We really wanted our son to feel comfortable enough to have his dad be there for him as well as, not to mention, having my needs met.

Kathy Gordon (Senior Instructor/Trainer with Hand in Hand Parenting) gave us a wonderful tool when she was a guest speaker for FLV. She suggested that in order for my son to see me and feel safe enough for his daddy to put him to sleep, I should stay inside the room by the bedroom door while my son's dad stayed and listened to our son. And then each night, slowly but surely, remove myself from the room until he completely felt secure enough with his daddy putting him to sleep.

So the following night, after setting the stage (again, a tool that I will discuss more in Chapter Eight) by letting our son know that Daddy would be the one to put him to sleep, his dad starting practicing the Time In tool with our son on the bed, while I stood by the door. The first night was a bit rough, as our son was crying and flailing his body around. His dad gently explained that he was going to be there to protect both of them from getting hurt and reassured him that he was safe with daddy.

During the entire time, I stayed inside the bedroom standing by the door, also gently reconfirming him that he was safe with daddy. This allowed our son to feel secure, knowing that I wasn't going anywhere and that daddy could also be there for him to get through his flooded feelings.

After a couple of nights of doing this, I was able to get from being in the bedroom to sitting in the hallway with the bedroom door open so he could see me whenever he wanted to (which normally would only last about ten to fifteen minutes before he would fall asleep). Then after a couple of nights of me having one foot in the office and one foot in the hallway, he soon felt completely comfortable with me closing the bedroom door and going into the office.

It worked! It was a miracle! The whole duration took about a week. It was well worth it and had been such a huge shift in all of us being able to get our needs met. Because his dad was able to be a loving and patient anchor for our son, it allowed our son to get through his feelings and trust in his dad to be fully present and gentle, yet setting a healthy boundary (which I will talk more about in Chapter Nine). Not to mention the bond between the two of them had strengthened immensely!

Now if I would've just ignored my son's fear around not having me put him to sleep and just having him "deal with" his daddy doing this task rather than both of us being present with practicing Time In, it probably would've taken a lot longer than a week for him to transition with feeling safe enough without me having to always be there when he goes to bed.

Now that you have an idea of how Time In works, let's move onto the next piece of the Triad, Playlistening.

PlayListening

In a world of "Don'ts" and "No's," it can be pretty frustrating for a child who wants to explore his world from a pure lens of creativity.

Our society has put so much focus on children's education and learning that I feel it is beginning to diminish our children's creative spirit and potential. As more and more tests and homework are being assigned, it is becoming more difficult for children to have an outlet through creative play. Even children in kindergarten are getting more tests–for what reason a five year-old needs to do homework and take tests continues to puzzle me.

I'm a huge fan of Alfie Kohn, author of "Unconditional Parenting" whom speaks passionately about human behavior, education, and parenting. I am fascinated and inspired by his insight on these very topics. He enthusiastically challenges the wisdom of the traditional school system and paves the way for parents to ponder on revolutionizing education beyond standardized tests, grades, and homework.

Don't get me wrong, learning is an important part of a child's development, but it is not the only essential key to a happy and successful life. And before our children step out into the "real world," how we communicate and connect with them is vital. Of course, the "real world" is not some outward place that our children will one day be thrown into. The real world is what is now going on within the walls of your home. How are you relating to your children currently? How are you communicating or not communicating with them? And are you being able to, as Pam Leo put its, fill your own "love cup" in the process (as in getting your own needs met)?

They say laughter is the best medicine. I completely agree – especially when it comes to children's laughter. And when parents are actively engaging in play that brings about giggles and shrieks of joy, it ignites more connection.

Imagination and play for children plays (yes, pun intended) an essential role in their development that helps to expand their cognitive, physical, social and emotional well-being. Education does not have to be confined within a classroom; in fact, play is the best way for children to learn, process and soak in knowledge through their experiences.

In retrospect, it plays an important role for our own development as parents, as well. Children can actually help us adults bring out the laughter and play within ourselves.

> *"Follow the giggles,"* says Lawrence J. Cohen, author of Playful Parenting. *"When we get disconnected from children*

– and we do, again and again – play is our best bridge back to deep connection with them."

Before I had our son, I wouldn't say I was the best at getting children to laugh or even to want to play with me. I actually found it challenging to connect with children. As shocking as it was, what with me being an advocate in connection and forming Family Love Village (which is all about connecting families together), I just didn't know how to fully engage in a child's world. Even in the early stages of being a new mother, I found it, at times, quite challenging to relate to play that made it fun for kids. I was more of the nurturer type (well, I still am), and I really wasn't one who would get down on my knees and wrestle with the kids.

It wasn't until I came across Lawrence J. Cohen's book, Playful Parenting, as well as a technique called Playlistening by Patty Wipfler that I felt the confidence to tap into my inner child and I was able to interact in more fun ways. Not every parent has this gift - unlike my son's dad who has this extraordinary innate ability to naturally connect with children (and animals) where they feel drawn to his presence. He definitely has a gift with making children laugh and make play fun and interactive.

In this portion of this chapter, I'll be sharing the Playlistening tool, what it can look like and how is it beneficial in helping to create connection while simultaneously being able to actively listen when the child gets off-kilter.

The following are guidelines for this type of play:

- ***Allow It To Be Child-led*** – During this form of play, follow your child's lead. Let your child be in charge. This allows your child to feel more confident in her choices and gives her the freedom to learn what she is looking to discover. It gives us parents the chance to give our undivided attention that children truly crave. It also makes the child feel heard and understood which can increase self-esteem and lets the child know that their choices and opinions count within the family.

- ***Take On the Less Powerful Role*** – A lot of times children feel extremely intimidated in the world; allowing them to be in the more dominant role...to feel more powerful, stronger, and more clever in this form of play...can help them to process some of the fears and tension around being small. By you being the less competent, less smart and more of the fumbling "fool," this allows them to laugh and feel more confident in their ability to move through any challenges they might be struggling with.

- ***Promote As Much Laughter as You Can*** – This allows for a more serious situation to become more playful. This can be through roughhousing (again where the child is in the more powerful lead), through laughter and by you pretending to make silly mistakes (i.e. pretend to fumble and fall while your child is chasing you), or anything silly that will spark the giggles! Sometimes, as parents, we are too serious and just want to get things done right away, but this can lead to power struggles and disconnection.

Here's a great example by Patty that can make a power struggle with trying to get your child ready to get out of the house less stressful and more fun:

> *"If your child refuses to put her jacket on, you might playfully get down on your hands and knees, pull at her shirttail, and say, "Oh, Pleeeease! Just touch your jacket before we go outside!" Your child will probably giggle, crow "No! Not even a touch!" and run away. You can lumber after her, begging pitifully, while she laughs away the stresses that created the power struggle with you. After a few minutes of allowing her the upper hand, she is more likely to be able to choose to put on her jacket."*

- ***Actively Listen and Observe for Any Upsets During This Time*** – Sometimes during the laughter and physical play, children's frustrations that they may be working through could arise, which can cause them to start crying or have big feelings for no apparent reason (or so you think). Or perhaps the physical play with them overpowering you turns into them really wanting to hurt you (unintentionally) in an effort to relieve any tension or heal past unresolved hurts that have been storing and brewing inside of them throughout the day.

Sometimes you may not even be wrestling with them for the physicality of them needing to release any old hurts to come out. Sometimes it could be something as simple as you throwing a ball at your child to catch. Then all of a sudden, you notice your daughter getting upset as she throws the ball at you swiftly with force behind it. Instead of you reacting and getting upset, you could fumble backwards, surprised, which could lead to a few giggles that will most likely encourage them to keep throwing the ball towards you in order to laugh some more.

Through using this technique, it allows situations that would be a bit more serious to become more light and fun. And just like with Time In, it creates connection that allows the child to feel supported, which can return her back into her loving self, renewed and ready to go on to the next thing the family has planned for the day.

Now that you've learned about the second leg to the triad of connection, we will now discuss the third one called Special Time.

Special Time

Time In and Playlistening can build a significant amount of connection with your child. Yet there is one more piece to the puzzle that is necessary for a strong bond and that is through special one-on-one time together.

Besides the obvious of establishing a conscious kinship with your child, there are many benefits to having Special Time with your child. Some of the reasons would be:

- Helps your child conquer their fears

- Lets him/her feel important and accepted as this form of connection is child-led

- Allows you to become more present and engage in what your child is interested in

- Builds trust, warmth and fun

- Models flexibility and cooperation so that your child can learn these qualities, as well

Here are several guidelines in using this technique:

- *Announce Special Time* – It's crucial for your child to know the difference between regular play and Special Time as they will know this to be uninterrupted time spent with you. You could also give Special Time a special name, as well. Perhaps your child's name (i.e. *"Let's have some Angie Time"*).

- *Allow It To Be Child-led* – Just as with Playlistening, Special Time is whatever your child wants to do (of course, within range of safety for everyone involved). It gives her the chance to direct you, for a change. This also entails being open to doing whatever the child wants to do. For example, she may want to take all the books down and ask you to put them all back. You could then be playful and stack them backwards or on your head. Or perhaps your child asks you to take all of his toys out of the toy bin and tells you to re-arrange it or to put the toys all over the room. You could playfully pretend that you don't want to and beg him not to make you. This could then turn into Playlistening as he laughs and works through her feelings of always being told what to do. But now, the tables have turned and she is telling you what to do in a light and fun manner.

    And although this is child-led, it doesn't mean that you can't set healthy boundaries around Special Time. There are times when this is a necessity.

For instance, whenever I mention Special Time to my son, majority of the time he wants to watch a show or play a game on the computer. So when I ask and/or announce Special Time, I sometimes set a healthy boundary that we can have Special Time and do whatever he wants besides media. Sometimes he gets upset and has big feelings, which gives a great opportunity to do Time In so that he can release his emotions. Other times, he is more accepting of this option and then proceeds to let me know what he would like to do during this time. And then there may be days that I do agree to media being the vehicle for his special one-on-one time. It just depends on what feels organically in the flow for our family. There are no strict rules to conscious parenting. It is whatever is feeling true for your family dynamic. These are merely guidelines and tools that have helped many families with creating connection.

- *Put a Timer On It* – This is important so they know that Special Time is for a limited time before going about the day or before getting ready for bed, for example. It can be however long you announce it to be. It can be as brief as ten minutes to as long as an hour (it's really dependent on how much time you have throughout your day). I have found whether it's ten minutes or twenty minutes, no matter what, it has helped the relationship with my son grow even closer.

- *Be Fully Present* – When you are focused and really present, it reassures your child that she matters. Being fully present means turning off your TV, the computer and your phone (or at least put it on silent during this time). This means you are in it to win it (in this case, the connection)! And no, this doesn't mean that it's okay to put the timer on pause for a moment to answer an important phone call or text either! It's really imperative that she knows she has your undivided attention and you are engaged in whatever holds her interest.

- *Prepare for Big Feelings* – A lot of times children don't want Special Time to end (let alone any type of play). Can you blame them? So when Special Time is over, they may tend to have big feelings about it. This is when the Time In and Playlistening tools can come in handy.

Here's a secret to preparing yourself for big feelings. Let's say you and your family have to leave for an outing or you have to cook dinner; what you can do is tell your child that you both will have 10-20 minutes of Special Time. Then of course, set the stage and let him/her know that after Special Time is over, you all have to get going out the door or you have to prepare dinner (or whatever the task might be at hand). But in your head, you would schedule a total of 30-40 minutes altogether so that it allots at least twenty minutes for Time In, in case he/she ends up having flooded feelings. Big feelings may or may not arise, but when you give them the time to not only be present for just the fun parts, but to also be there during the heartache of Special Time being over, it will help them to re-regulate.

To recap, there are three wonderful tools that can activate reciprocity between you and your child. They are Time-In, Playlistening and Special Time. When you combine all of these together, you are likely to find that your child is more willing to trust in your capability to help him work through his emotions more easily, to be more open to cooperating and have more fun together.

Next, we will talk about validation and why being heard and understood is central to communicating consciously with your child and with the whole family. Turn the page to understand its importance.

Chapter Seven:
Why is Validation So Vital?

"Love is saying 'I feel differently' instead of 'You're wrong'."
~ Unknown

What does it mean to be validated? To validate means that your feelings, thoughts, and/or ideas are accepted. Validating someone not only means that you accept the feelings, thoughts, and/or ideas, it means that you are willing to understand and nurture them, as well. And just like the quote above, raising your child in a loving environment doesn't necessarily mean you won't have a different opinion about certain things (we all are entitled to our thoughts and feelings, after all). With validation, it means that you are being open to your child's thoughts and feelings without making him/her out to be "wrong" or "bad."

Now invalidation is when you are told that your emotions, thoughts, and/or ideas are unacceptable or irrational. They are rejected, ignored, or judged. Invalidating someone means that their behavior is inappropriate and should be hidden and/or not expressed.

It is critical to build and nurture open, honest communication with our kids by truly listening to them. By validating how our children feel, we are building trust and increasing their sense of self-worth.

Before my son was born, I had been doing a lot of research. Research on home births, co-sleeping, breast-feeding, attachment parenting, cloth diapering, organic bedding, you name it. My son's dad and I wanted to create the most conscious, sustainable, natural and non-toxic way to bring our son into the world.

Once our son was born, the next natural step to me was to find tools and resources on how to guide our son in the most loving and nurturing way that encourages connection. After all, there is no handbook that is given to new parents on how to become one (or so I thought at the time)! Plus, living next door to a mother, who used yelling as a way to communicate to her children, activated me into motion to find something close enough to a manual.

And that's when I discovered the reputable book, *Connection Parenting* by Pam Leo. I continue to highlight and share my gratitude towards this book, because this was the seedling that planted the concept of a "family love gathering" that soon sprouted into what Family Love Village is today.

One of the topics discussed in the book is how invalidating your child's feelings can create disconnection. It is not only mentioned in this book, but is also a basis for philosophies such as Emotional Intelligence and other inspiring resources.

These resources share how invalidation not only causes disconnection between the parent and the child, but can also cause the child to detach from how they process their feelings, which can, unfortunately, continue on into adulthood.

The following key points I will be sharing in this chapter are:

- What happens when a child feels invalidated
- Examples of invalidation
- Strategies to help children feel supported

Children can't help but feel their feelings. When we stop them from expressing their feelings, what they might end up feeling is a sense of rejection, unworthiness, and that something is "wrong" with them. Thus, they tend to hide, store, and/or push down their feelings, which not only causes disconnection in that present moment, but also can cause them to no longer confide in their parents, as they get older.

Children have the most purist form of creativity, and their job is to work through their discoveries, challenges, and triumphs through play and imagination. Unfortunately, I often witness adults in our society constantly diminishing their children's playful spirits.

Below are some examples of how adults tend to invalidate, including solutions that can be used instead.

Example 1: *"Stop being such a baby! There's nothing to be afraid of!"*

Solution: *"I understand you're feeling afraid. Tell me what's happening to make you scared."*

Example 2: *"Oh she's fine! It's just a little scratch. She's just being a cry baby."*

Solution: *"I see you hurt yourself. I'll comfort you until you feel better."*

What inspired me to write about this topic was a conversation that my son had with his nanny several years back about him seeing ghosts. I wasn't alarmed in the least. In fact, when I heard the story, I was very touched.

It was, indeed, quite the charming conversation that went as follows:

Son: *"You know ghosts only come out in the dark? They don't like light."*

Nanny: *"Who told you about ghosts?"*

Son: *"My spirit within me."*

Nanny: *"Are the spirits kind to you?"*

Son: *"Yeah."*

Nanny: *"Do they visit you?"*

Son: *"Yeah."*

The whole point of bringing up this conversation is because, in most cases, parents would most likely feel uncomfortable with the thought of their child talking to ghosts. And in most cases they would even say what their child is experiencing is ridiculous or silly–that ghosts aren't real, and possibly even go as far as getting upset with their child for talking about that nonsense.

Well, ghosts aren't the only things that can make a parent want to undermine a child's experiences. And, unfortunately, it usually happens in the day-to-day emotions that a child feels.

Some examples can be:

1. **When a child cries.**

   From the time a baby is born, the normal reaction for when an infant cries is to gently shush them. I think as adults, we are uncomfortable with the general emotion of crying, especially when we hear a baby cry. What tends to be the normal reaction is to try and calm them down. As a sidenote and a reminder from previous chapters, crying it out is not recommended. The main point of this particular topic about when a baby cries is that we tend to have an automatic response to want to shush their cries. It is just an observation on my end with what we tend to do. Well, as the child continues to grow and continues to explore their world, emotions and reactions can get more intense. Unfortunately, some adults may tend to think the child is overreacting and feel the urge to say, *"Calm down. There's nothing to cry about."* Have you noticed that even as adults, we tend to try and "soothe" other adults by saying, *"Don't cry. It's ok."* Yet crying is a healthy release that can get rid of toxins according to studies and is very much needed in order to self-regulate the brain.

2. **When a child gets injured.**

   The initial reaction for most parents is to want to reassure the child and make the pain go away which is normal. A common phrase that most adults say when they see a child fall down or hurt themselves is, *"Oh, you're ok. It's ok. You're fine."* Well, if you got injured, think about how annoying it is for someone to tell you that you're ok? I'm sure the reaction would be the same and would sound more like *"Um, actually that frickin' hurt! Don't tell me I'm fine when I'm not!"* Well the same thing could be happening to your child and can cause confusion for her because what she is feeling *is* painful, yet they're being told otherwise, which teaches the child to ignore their feelings and to basically numb the pain.

3. **When a child is scared.**

   Whether a child is scared of the dark because of a "monster underneath the bed" or scared when an adult is pretending to be a monster, a lot of times adults tend to discredit the child's fear by saying things like, *"There's nothing to be afraid of"* or *"I was just playing. Stop being such a scaredy cat!"*

4. **When a child is angry.**

   When a parent sees a child expressing anger, it can be uncomfortable for the adult to see their sweet, loving child this upset; especially when their child begins to hit, scratch, bite, and/or kick others. In most cases, the child is usually reprimanded for their actions; and, unfortunately, their feelings of rage are still festering within without a healthy release.

5. **When a child is sad.**

   Just as a parent doesn't like to see their child angry, the same goes for not wanting to see her sad. Yet even when they are sad, we want to ensure we refrain from invalidating them – even if you think telling them they are "fine" or "okay" will make them feel better. I'm going to use my son for an example here. He had done something that he had been asked several times before not to do. Unfortunately, during play, he forgot and his excitement took over and he did it anyways. There was a boundary set around it (which I will go into later in the book) and he felt sad. And although we had re-connected, he expressed to me that he felt he was a bully and a bad boy. Naturally, we don't want our children to feel like they are bad people that are bullies nor do we want them turning into bullies, either. So my first reaction was to console him and tell him he's not a bad boy or a bully; that he just made a mistake. What I thought was helping him feel better, was actually making him feel worse. What I didn't realize in this moment is that I was invalidating his feelings.

A dear friend of mine, Leigh Sietsema, who teaches "Quality Parenting" workshops to families, suggested I take another approach. So even though we had reconnected several hours earlier, it was yet another opportunity for us to connect deeper in order to ensure that everyone felt heard and validated. So the conversation went something like this:

Me: *"Son, you know how earlier you said you feel like a bad boy and a bully and I kept saying you weren't?"*

Son: *"Yeah. I still feel like I am though."*

Me: *"I wanted to let you know that I realized now that I was disregarding your feelings and I'm sorry."*

Son: *"It's ok. But I'm still a bad boy. And it wasn't really me that did it! It was the evil pterodactyl that got out of its cage in my brain and did it."*

Me: *"Ahhh! I get it that you feel like it wasn't really you. When I get frustrated and out of my center, I too feel like it's not who I really am. But it is still a part of us and when we make a mistake, we just want to make sure that we recognize and take responsibility for our mistakes. We've all made mistakes before, it's just a matter of owning up to it and learning from our mistakes."*

Son: *"Ok. I'm sorry."*

Me: *"It's ok. I also wanted to let you know that I've seen when you are kind and caring. I've seen when a friend of yours gets hurt and you check up on them to make sure they are ok. That's how I know you're not a bully or a bad boy. When I've brought grocery bags out of the car, you have voluntarily helped me without me even asking for help. Can you think of any other times that you care?"*

He went on to share more ways throughout the night about times that he was compassionate and loving. Not only was I able to go back to him and acknowledge that I invalidated him, (which models to him that even us adults make mistakes and that I was able to take ownership of what I did) but I was also able to help him regain his confidence in who he truly is and how he feels about himself.

As taught in the Quality Parenting workshops mentioned above (based on the book "Bring Out the Best in Your Child and Your Self" by Ilene Val-Essen), what I was doing was "watering the flowers" rather than the weeds. What this means is I was focusing on all the positive qualities about my son that nurtures the best within him instead of pointing out things that are "wrong" with him.

As mentioned above, when we don't allow children the opportunity to express their emotions, we are disabling them to truly feel. As a result, what children are really hearing from us is that they are not valid, not worthy and perhaps not even lovable. What ends up happening is children learn to hide their feelings. Children learn that they can no longer trust in our ability, as their parents, to keep them safe or to be heard and understood. This not only causes disconnection from us, but from their own innate ability to feel, which can later cause them to numb their feelings in adulthood.

List 3 ways you experienced feeling invalidated? Were you a child/teen or an adult? How did this make you feel?

_____
_____
_____
_____
_____
_____
_____
_____
_____
_____
_____
_____

So, what are some examples of ways we can show our children they can trust in us to support them through challenging moments?

Here are a few examples of phrases to guide children with feeling validated and supported:

1. ***"Let it all out."***

   My son's dad and I have been saying this to our son since he was very young. By allowing him the space to let out his feelings, he feels safe knowing he is being supported and comforted through the tears. When children are given the opportunity to cry while an adult is comforting them, they can more easily shed their grief.

2. ***"That must've hurt. I can see that you're sad. I'll be here to comfort you. Can you think of some ways that you can feel better?"***

   This allows the child to know that you understand she's hurting; and by asking her how she can make it feel better, it gives her a chance to find ways to heal, self-soothe, and develop problem-solving skills - while being reassured that you are by her side without trying to always "fix" the issue. As adults, we tend to feel uncomfortable with allowing children to experience their full range of emotions because we weren't allowed to growing up. So what we end up wanting to do is "fix" things for our children. Instead of focusing on what needs to be fixed, improved, or changed for your child and/or the situation due to it making you feel uneasy, focus on what really matters - the connection between you and your child without having to have an agenda of how you want the outcome to be is what is most important here.

3. *"It must've been scary seeing me act like a monster. I see that it upset you. What other games would you like to play?"*

This lets the child know that you are empathetic to his feelings, and asking him what he would rather do brings child-led play into effect. As a side note, pretending to be a monster, especially for toddlers, inflicts fear. Imagine you're the size of your child and how scary it must feel seeing a big body coming after her, while making scary faces. Patty Wipfler touches upon this topic more in her book, Playlistening.

4. *"You're really mad! I can see that you're upset at your younger sister for taking your toy. We don't hit in our family. Let's find a way to release your anger in a healthy way."*

One important factor with validating, when a child is angry, is to meet your child where they are at. What this means is, if she is angry, then a great way to help her know that her feelings matter and are accepted is by you reassuring her that sometimes mommy and daddy get just as upset, too. Meeting her with the same degree of frustration allows her to know that it's ok for her to have these emotions and that there are healthy ways to release them, too.

Meeting her at her level of emotion does NOT mean you should raise your voice. Nor does it mean you should belittle by making such comments as, "Oh she'll get over it" while patting her on the head. To meet your child where she is at is a gesture to help your child know that you know how it feels to be angry by saying,

> *"You're really mad! And it's okay to be mad. I get mad too. But we need to make sure that everyone's bodies are safe."*

There are many approaches to releasing the anger in a healthy way. Some examples could be writing, drawing, storytelling, ripping up paper, kneading play dough or clay or even getting physically active, such as running, dancing or doing jumping jacks. For my son, what worked when he was younger was a game we called the "Sea Monster" where he would chase after me and pretend to tie me up then he would go and hide. After a minute or so, I would "free" myself and begin to look for him. When I got close to where he was hiding, he would jump out, scare me and chase me again. This was a form of Playlistening where he felt in control and helped him to work through his feelings.

Another great tool is counting down from ten to one together. No this is not the common strategy that some parents use to count to three "or else!" The purpose for counting from ten to one is to allow your child to calm his nerves as he counts down. I have actually found this to be very helpful when calming my own nerves, as well.

My son and I even made a "Magic Healing Box" where he kept a crystal, rose quartz, sage, paper and a purple crayon (his favorite color at the time), so he can look inside to choose what could help him through his frustrations.

The more options you offer your child, the more easily you and your child can come up with ideas to come back to center and self-soothe.

One great tool I've witnessed helping is what I like to call "Ice Grenades." Leigh Sietsema, shared this exercise with me. She learned it along her conscious parenting journey, and it has helped her six children through their big feelings.

Whenever you start to notice your child's heat starting to boil over and about to become a ticking time bomb to physically explode onto himself or loved ones, help lead your child to regulate those feelings by releasing those emotions by throwing ice outside at a wall instead.

I hate to admit it, but I was known in the past to be a "slammer," meaning whenever I used to get upset I would slam doors. I'm sure most parents can relate to the annoying sound of their teenage kids slamming doors. As unhealthy as it was and definitely not condoning it, slamming a door was my own way of releasing the tension and anger built up inside.

Throwing "ice grenades" can be just as effective with releasing the pent-up feelings, and it's a much healthier way for you and your child/teenager to offload.

Below are some instructions on what to do:
- Get a bucket or bowl and fill it up with ice
- Find an accessible empty wall outside of your house without any windows near it
- Optional: get chalk and either you or your child, if she wants to, can draw a symbol that reflects what she is upset about
- Then encourage her to throw the ice at the wall and/or the drawing (if a symbol or picture was drawn)
- Allow her to yell or express her anger about how she feels around the situation
- If you are just as frustrated, you can join in with releasing your own ticking time bombs, as well
- More than likely, what will end up happening is that the underlying feeling will arise–which is usually about feeling sad or scared
- Continue to be there to move through the feelings until she (and you) have been able to re-center yourselves

In addition to the above tools mentioned, another way to validate our children that reassures them that we are fully engaged and understand where they are coming from is called Reflective Listening. This is where you are truly present and able to tune into what your child is saying to you. You then empathetically state, in your own words, what you heard them express. This not only allows them to feel heard and understood, it quite often gives them the opportunity to further explore their feelings - which can also reveal the underlying root cause of their frustration. This form of listening allows you and your child to go deeper with respectful communication that can help to defuse an uncomfortable situation while teaching them how to articulate how they are feeling. Reflective listening is an art form; it is an empathetic language that inspires mutual respect not just with growing our relationships with our children but also helps with growing our relationships with other family members, friends, and colleagues – personally and professionally.

So whether it's being supportive and developing trust as our children go through their emotions, or perhaps sharing about a strange topic (such as ghosts), the more we are able to come from a genuine place of compassion and understanding towards our children's needs, upsets and fears, the more we are able to stay connected to our children.

I highly recommend this very insightful book that goes into explicit detail that has wonderful examples. It includes easy to understand cartoons and exercises on how to help validate our children's feelings and uses alternatives to punishment all the while creating connection. It is called "How To Talk So Kids Will Listen & Listen So Kids Will Talk" by Adele Faber and Elaine Mazlish. This has been monumental for me with continuing to validate both me and my son's feelings while finding more respectful ways to communicate to one another.

So to sum things up, when we become the observer and ask questions while authentically listening and meeting our children where they are at compassionately, we are able to create more connection with our children. Thus, we are embedding more harmony within the home, while raising emotionally healthy, compassionate, and confident adults.

In the following chapter, we will outline how change can affect children's behavior and ways that can better prepare them through the shifting waves between the highs and lows of emotions during change.

Chapter Eight:
From Caterpillar to Butterfly: What Helps Through Transitions?

"If nothing ever changed, there'd be no butterflies"
~ Author Unknown

Change can be an exciting and riveting experience that brings up feelings of curiosity and anticipation. Yet it can also get tarnished with emotions of fear, anxiety and uncertainty of the unknown. Studies have shown that our experiences (whether enjoyable or unpleasant), even from birth, can continue to linger in our memory and be triggered in similar situations we encounter as we get older. And although change is inevitable, it doesn't mean it's accepted at all times in all ways–especially in the eyes of a child.

When we're in a hurry to get out of the house, we adults tend to expect our children just to get up and follow suit when we say, *"Let's go!"* Sometimes our tunnel vision and narrow-minded focus of our own to-do lists and agendas become more important than the play and work that our children are doing. Unfortunately, our needs and priorities seem to disregard what our children are focused on, and our children can quickly pick up on this and can get the raw end of the stick. We often rush them out of their own space and expect them to cooperate into ours, as if what they are doing is irrelevant.

It's very similar to what I had mentioned in Chapter Three about communicating to your baby/toddler that you are picking him up, so as to let him know that you respect his body and world. It goes back to the question that I will repeat here: *"How would you feel if someone picked you up unexpectedly while you were focused on something?"* If your answer is "shocked," "upset" or "uncomfortable," the same could be going through your child's mind, especially if he/she is absorbed in play. So to relate it to the concept of empathetically getting your child to transition from one activity to another, you could also ask yourself, *"How would I feel if someone interrupted me in the middle of something that I was doing creatively and was trying to hurriedly rush me away from what I was happily doing?"*

It takes time for children to transition from one activity to another. They need this time, and it would behoove us to honor that time and find ways to support our children through this process.

In this chapter, I will share the following topics:

- Examples of change that may cause stress for children

- How transitions can affect children

- Strategies on how you and your child can adjust to change more easily

- The importance of Rites of Passage

- How media continues to play a role in how society has been raising our boys and girls and what needs to shift

Our ability to manage change is a critical element for our mental well-being. It embodies each of our individual traits that get developed through a fusion of events that occur in each stage of our lives, the seasons of nature, as well as how nurturing our environment is. Children can either experience loving, consistent support from parents/adults or they can experience family members or authoritative figures that are unsupportive and blindly insensitive to their emotional needs. And then there can be moments where they experience a little bit of both. Let's be honest here, parenting can be challenging let alone taking the time to actually do it consciously! But the more we practice this way of communicating and relating to our children, the deeper the connection that can be made within our families.

So back to the topic at hand: CHANGE! It can be very challenging for children to be able to trust in adults and simultaneously for us to be able to handle their flooded feelings during transitions and change. For some children, it is difficult for them to ask for our help when dealing with a new situation. For others, they may end up coping by constantly yearning for our attention. And then for some, it may seem like they're handling the shift just fine, but deep inside they are struggling. Thus, big feelings may occur suddenly out of nowhere.

There are various reasons that can cause distress when it comes to change. Several examples are:

- A new sibling
- Separation from parents
- Starting daycare or pre-school
- Changing schools or teachers
- Divorce/Separation
- Illness or death of a family member
- Having to grow up too fast to take care of someone who is ill
- Moving to a new home
- Changing friends
- Diagnosis of illness or disability of child
- Puberty
- New step-parents
- Foster parents

Research shows that transition can be just as stressful for children as it can be for adults. The result of stress can have significant effects on children's emotional well-being and ability to learn. For instance, they can either become withdrawn or just the opposite and become clingy. Irrational and aggressive behavior may occur, as well. They also may acquire sleep issues, appetite loss and may have difficulty with focusing on learning. Coping with change can be a challenge and sometimes the parent could also experience a child and/or teen who becomes rebellious and doesn't want to listen or perhaps will do anything to get attention (even if it's "bad" attention, it is still attention that they are getting).

And while helping to prepare your child for the change is critical, there are no guarantees that a smooth transition will happen. It's also not always easy trying to figure out if a child will cope well with change. And a lot of the time, the change can be hidden in their behaviors, where some behaviors that might be considered "normal milestones" might actually be the cause of traumatic change. For instance, I have witnessed on two separate occasions with two different children around the same age of two to three years old, whom you would think were going through the normal milestone of saying *"Mine!"* to every toy. But when they are saying *"Mine"* to the refrigerator and *"Mine!"* and pointing to their mommy, one must ponder on whether their circumstance of moving from home to home is making them feel insecure about their situation and feeling the need to claim to other children what is theirs. This last part is in no way a professional standpoint. It is just my own personal pondering and observations.

So, as an ever-evolving parent, being open, supportive and patient is highly suggested, as you and your child may adjust to change differently and at different times. The more you are able to tap into being an empathetic and compassionate caregiver, the better chance your child will adapt much quicker to change.

Do your best to gently remind yourself and your child that change is a necessary part of life. It propels us to move forward, to expand our awareness and be able to acclimate to new situations.

There are several ways that can help children to transition easier.

- ***Create a Rhythm*** - For children, rituals and rhythms of the day can be extremely important. And when there has been a shift, whether small or major, it helps to create a rhythm to help stabilize the trauma around changes. Children tend to thrive in familiar and consistent surroundings. It gives them a sense of security, reassurance and safety in knowing what is going to happen next and to be able to rely on a rhythm throughout the day. But even in the midst of familiar rhythms, change happens and it happens all the time. And as long as there is an adult who is able to lovingly guide a child through the changes with supportive tools, the transition can be accepted more easily.

  Some examples that can create a rhythm are family meal times, scheduled times throughout the day to do Special Time (for instance, once in the morning, once in the afternoon and once after dinner, if you are able to) as well as bedtime stories at night.

  Other rhythms could be a family tradition that you do during mealtimes. For instance, in our family, after we send loving energy and prayers to our food, we have a special thing we do that we call "Gratitude Share" where each of us shares at least one thing that we are grateful for that happened that day or in that moment. Whatever the case may be, find what resonates with your own family values and begin the rhythm to help your child through changes.

- ***Set the Stage*** - This is where you explain to your child (in an upbeat manner) what is going to happen before it happens. This allows him/her to prepare for what is to come. I learned this tool from Jessica Maria Hicks, M.A. Depth Pscyhology (when she was a guest speaker for FLV).

  > *"So let's say you need to take your child to the dentist's office. You can set the stage by saying, "Tomorrow we are going to the dentist's office. We may be in the waiting room for a little bit until the dentist is ready to see us. While we're waiting we can read some books or bring some small toys to quietly play. And*

then we're going to go inside his office and the dentist is going to check your teeth."

What you are doing here is basically walking them through what will happen by giving them a frame of reference. It may not be the whole story of what will happen, but it's the frame.

Another way to set the stage is by being an inquisitive parent. For example: *"So let's say we're at the dentist and you get upset and decide that you want to leave before you get your regular checkup. Would that be helpful or not helpful?"* Then the child could answer *"Not helpful." "And then if we are reading a book and then suddenly you throw the book angrily, would that create connection or disconnection?" "Disconnection."*

This is a great way of letting off your own steam of how frustrating it is when those things do happen. You can also make it light and fun with how you ask. This not only gives them a chance to laugh, but it also allows them to see how being unhelpful it can be if they end up getting dysregulated at the dentist office. The same applies to grocery shopping or any time your family is going on an outing.

Of course, it doesn't mean your child won't go through any upset feelings, because you can never determine what lies ahead (only within the present moment). But setting the stage can help get through changes more smoothly, because they know what to expect, which, as mentioned above, is an important part of their rhythm.

- **Have fun -** When parents need to get out of the house or have their own agendas to get things done, they become unconscious to the fact of how they're emitting their energy. Children can be very sensitive to our body language, our facial expressions, the tone of voice and if our behavior is erratic when trying to get everyone out of the house in a hurry. So the more that you can make it fun, the more chances you'll experience your child being able to cooperate a lot easier. Some great examples could be pretending to be in a parade while marching to the car, having your child hold onto your waist as you slide them across the floor to the front door or being monkeys while giving them a piggy back ride to their car seat. This goes back to the point of Playlistening that I mentioned in Chapter Six – the sillier you are and the more ways you can incorporate fun, the more cooperation you will get from your child. And the easier things can flow for the rest of your day together when you start off on the right track.

- ***Manage Your Time*** - In addition to having fun, it is also a good idea to allot enough time for the transition from one activity to another. I know this can be a difficult one to acquire for most parents. Heck, it is one I am constantly needing to practice every day! But if you can prepare yourself by getting up earlier to get breakfast and lunch ready (or have lunch ready the night before) and give you and your family ample time to get out of the house, the transition can be much smoother. This is as much of a reminder for my readers as it is for me! Trust me on this one!

- ***Write a Book*** - Writing a book for your child can be beneficial with helping to introduce a situation that can be challenging or scary to experience for the first time. I first learned about this through Ruth Beaglehole's 6-week parenting course that my son's dad and I took several years ago.

It doesn't have to be a complicated or extravagant book either. Heck, if my son's dad wasn't such a talented artist, I probably would've been drawing stick figures (Oh wait, I actually do!) You also don't have to be an eloquent writer, either. I just so happen to be a writer, but it definitely doesn't mean that you have to be an author to create a book for your child. It can be as easy as:

- Getting four to six blank pieces of paper and folding them in half

- Stapling the middle at the crease or punching three holes and tying a ribbon in each hole to hold the book together

- Writing a couple of sentences for each page

- Drawing a couple of pictures that flow with the words. If you're not much of an artist, that is okay. You can even pick out pictures of your family, cut out images in magazines or print some from the internet to glue in the book.

Then once you have finished creating the book, you can start reading it to your child. If there is a major transition, I would suggest making the book at least one to two weeks ahead of time so that you can give your child a chance to prepare for the change. A great example of this is when you are traveling out of town for business and it is your first time away, the first day of school, perhaps the first doctor's visit or even when you are introducing a new nanny to your child. Whatever the situation may be that could cause change to bring on discomfort on your child's behalf, writing a book to help your child feel safe and comforted through a challenging and/or scary experience is very valuable.

On the topic of writing, there is also a deeper process to help not only your child, but yourself, as well, move through a transition together as a family. Here's an excerpt from an article that Jessica Maria Hicks wrote for the FLVillage Crier:

1. Make space for your own feelings of grief, guilt, and sadness at needing to make a change. Write a letter to close this chapter. Outline what you have loved about your current paradigm, all the good memories, why it has worked for you thus far and what you will miss about it.

2. Tell your children that there is going to be a change and make space for their feelings. First, *"there is going to be a change and this current situation is coming to a close."* Next, allow space for all the children's feelings with love and compassion. Make space for your child's sadness, anger, resentment, and feeling powerless over the decision by listening with empathy and refrain from trying to convince or persuade them out of their feelings.

3. Memorialize the current situation. You can do this in a thoughtful and intentional way by offering:

   - a journaling session; you can follow dictation or your child can draw pictures

   - writing a book that illustrates & describes the current situation

   - writing a poem/ode to what you are leaving behind that you can print and frame

4. Present the new plan. Once you have processed your own feelings and allowed your children to grieve the old chapter and memorialized the current situation in a tangible place of honor, it is time to present the new paradigm. Lay out your expectations of the new plan with upbeat optimism.

By giving your child and/or teen a sacred place where all his/her feelings are valid and a ritual is created around the transition, it frees up the space for your child and/or teen to heal and adjust to change more easily.

Speaking of ritual, I wanted to also mention the importance of ceremony and stages of transition for our youth of today. Where technology and gadgets have replaced the wonder of nature and where rites of passage have been forgotten in our western society, as a conscious collective it would be ideal to celebrate and nurture our children coming of age, as did our ancestors.

Even with how our children enter the world, there is something magical to be expressed when we initiate through ritual. One of the most memorable moments when I was pregnant with my son was when we had a blessingway ceremony. Our family and friends each brought a special pendant that they gifted and had made into one single necklace that I could wear during labor. My midwife had given me a beautiful bottle that contained blessed water so that I could pour it into the birthing tub. Our loved ones painted rocks and shared the deeper meaning of the drawings that represented their loving intentions for our birth. Where meditation and drums filled the air and aromatherapy-infused water caressed my feet, this was the most blissful way to welcome our son into the world.

Of course birth is not the only celebration that marks a coming of age. There are ceremonies to mark transition from boyhood to manhood, girlhood to womanhood, as well as initiating when a person achieves status as an elder (also known as "croning"), including the transition of death, just to name a few. Our ancestors honored each of these stages, which also included the essence of Mother Earth. Unfortunately, they are but whispers in the wind, slowly drifting away. So it would be conducive for our soul connection if we were to once again embrace the intimate rhythms of nature and re-introduce ourselves to the art of ceremony.

An interesting and valid point that a friend of mine Verdarluz (author of "Codex of the Soul" and "Aquarius Dawns") made was that:

> *"Another effect of the lack of participatory rites of passage involves a subsequent psychological projection and transference of archetypal energies onto the child's activities. For instance, many children between the ages of 8 and 18 are enamored with violence through movies, sports and video games, yet few have experienced violent or life-threatening situations. The magnetic attraction toward violence is completely normal in understanding the archetypal forces at play in the child's psyche. However, since Western society has appropriated virtually no healthy containers for "the ritual experience of one's mortality," children must project this psychic need onto movie and video-game characters and sports "heroes."*

This brings up a good point on how children (especially boys) are seldom supported to find healthy ways to release their aggression. So what can we do to re-engage our children and ourselves in the art of ceremonial transitions that give our children a safe and sacred space to work through their emotions and learn important life lessons at the same time? The answer is to find ways to celebrate our children and teens in every stage of their development by also connecting to the natural world. We do this by creating a safe community for our children to participate in, as well as seeking and practicing compassionate ways to build up their self-esteem, self-love and confidence.

There are traditions that do celebrate children maturing into adulthood, such as Bar/Bat Mitzvahs, "Sweet 16" birthdays, and Quinceañeras. However, there is something to be said about getting back to our roots, intertwining with nature and commemorating our children like the indigenous people have done for so many centuries. Hunters learned how to craft tools such as nets and bows and arrows; gatherers knew which roots, nuts, seeds, fruit and greens were edible and when and where to find them. These hunter/gatherer children also knew how to navigate through their territory, build huts, make fires and cook. All of these ancient skills were acquired as a direct result of the rites of passage as these children celebrated the coming of age.

I'm not saying that families have to get rid of their technology, throw away their microwaves and start building fires from twigs and cook outside in a forest (although growing your own food, slow cooking on a stove vs. a meal in a can put in a microwave is definitely better for your health and taste buds). This just isn't realistic to most people in our society. But when you blend these cross-cultural traditions alongside each other along with sanctifying your child by moving through these paramount life lessons, it gives them an opportunity to experience self-worth and independence consciously.

Since we have been discussing the topic of change in this chapter, I feel there is a deep shift needing to take place with how society views boys/men and girls/women and how media has been playing such a significant role in this.

There are two impactful documentaries called "Miss Representation" and "The Mask You Live In" by filmmaker, Jennifer Siebel Newsom (also founder of The Presentation Project) that really goes into the stereotypes that our nation tends to get sucked into. This first film exposes how mainstream media and our culture can undermine the worth of women in our society; how media continues to objectify women for their looks and sensuality rather than seeing their potential as intelligent leaders. It also goes into how men are dominant in business and politics and how media is essentially brainwashing this form of untruthful duality about how women and men ought to behave that our children are unfortunately being exposed to.

The second film heart-wrenchingly uncovers the dilemma we have with the "tough love/boys don't cry/act like a 'real' man" mentality that limits boys' capability for empathy where they have to hide who they truly are in order to live up to society's expectations of who they "should" be. The misrepresentation that these children grow up in and how us adults are continuously allowing this to happen is hurting our civilization as a whole.

Paul Haggis, (Canadian director, screenwriter, and producer) in Miss Representation stated, *"We see the world in a certain way and we don't really challenge that often. And so we just replicate the world we grew up in without really asking why we are doing it."*

We are literally in a crisis with this recycled parenting old way of thinking. Something has to give; we need a shift. We cannot continue replicating this broken system of how we have been raising our children. We are in need of a social healing of the masculine and the feminine. We have to find a way to eliminate the price tag of power and greed and take a social collective stand by challenging the Media and Big Corporation Cartel (as I like to call it) by supporting conscious media, books, communities, as well as supporting local companies, humanely-raised animal farms, organic and non-GMO and discovering more ways to be sustainable that truly have our best interests, our children's best interests, and our planet's best interests at heart. And by taking a stand for your child with choosing to raise them with empathetic communication, mutual respect, and confidence can be the catalyst towards this evolution that is so needed in order for our society to thrive.

With that said, here is a quick review for this chapter. There are many examples of change that can cause stress for children and families.

How this change affects children can cause a direct experience of disconnection that parents, sometimes, aren't aware of. Creating a rhythm that children are familiar with on a daily basis, setting the stage to help ease the transition and by making books, as well as moving through the process together for your children and yourself, are wonderful tools to cope with change and help them feel more safe and secure within their environment. Also, integrating "coming of age" rituals helps our children to shift from the once reluctant caterpillar into a beautiful butterfly that feels confident with taking flight out into the "real" world.

As Katie Couric stated, *"The media can be an instrument of change. It can maintain the status quo and reflect the views of society. Or it can hopefully awaken people and change minds. I think it depends on who is piloting the plane."*

This too is reflective of our parenting and who is piloting the plane: whether it is the old views you once had or perhaps the awakened parent who is ready to create that shift within your home. The wheel is now in your hand. It is up to you to now steer it.

Now that you have a better understanding about just how imperative it is to be more aware of how change can affect our children's behavior and ways to aid them in transitioning, in the upcoming chapter I will be sharing how to find ways to work with your children while establishing boundaries without getting overheated with emotions.

CHAPTER NINE:
Is It Possible to Set Boundaries That Inspire Connection?

"Caring for children is a dance between setting appropriate limits as caretakers and avoiding unnecessary power struggles that result in unhappiness."
~ Charlotte Davis Kasl

Sometimes people get the wrong impression when it comes to conscious parenting. As mentioned earlier, some tend to think conscious parenting promotes passive parenting. This is not the case (at least within the pages of this book). Let's not confuse compassion and empathy with permissiveness.

In Chapter Three, we learned that permissive parenting seeks to heal past wounds from their upbringing by trying to be the "friend" rather than having to look like the "bad guy" while being in fear of losing the child's love. This is not to say a parent cannot create a beautiful friendship/kinship with their child. In the context with permissive parenting though, it can be harmful. Authoritarian parenting uses force, coercion, and bribes to get the child to do what the parent wants. This form of parenting can also invalidate the child's feelings and uses consequences as a way to place fear into the child in order to comply with the adult's commands. And although authoritarian parenting is on the polar end of permissive parenting, neither of these styles of parenting produce connection. As mentioned within the chapters of this book, it actually hinders the relationship and the bond.

So how do you set healthy boundaries that raise your child's confidence level without inflicting your own fears and self-limiting beliefs?

Within this chapter, I will raise the awareness on:

- What is scaffolding and why is it important?

- How to scaffold while keeping your cool during a melt-down

- Why natural consequences are better than coercive consequences and what are some alternatives

The term, "scaffolding" (coined by Ruth Beaglehole), expresses the sentiment behind what I believe truly reflects what we want to accomplish within our parenting. What comes to mind when you think of the term "scaffolding" might be of a base that holds up the infrastructure of a building. So when it comes to consciously parenting, scaffolding can be thought of as a web of boundaries with conscious intention that supports the framework of the relationship between you, your child, and the world. Whereas the mere word "limit" has a negative connotation, is inflexible and doesn't serve to inspire success, it serves to control. If you look up the definition for the word "limit" it is to confine, restrain, and hinder.

I would like to shift our lens regarding the terminology and the perspective around the purpose of what "setting limits" serves. There needs to be healthy boundaries that help set up our children for success with their interactions in the world and within themselves. Rather than a boundary being seen as a means to control our child's behavior, it instead could be considered a pillar that strengthens the foundation – hence scaffolding.

Why is scaffolding so important? Why can it be so hard to stick with the boundary without giving in or using fear-based tricks? And why does it seem like our children continue to push those boundaries while pushing our buttons?

When we are scaffolding, we are helping our children to learn about self-regulation in order to be able to set boundaries for themselves. By scaffolding, you are sowing the seeds of respect and responsibility. Scaffolding in this context is, by nature, compassionate and inspires security and connection between child and parent. This doesn't mean a boundary can't be firm when necessary. There are times when we have to be firm but it doesn't mean we have to be harsh while doing so. When a child is growing within a network of scaffolding support and the necessity for strong safety boundaries arises, the child will be more receptive and respectful of the powerful energy behind the request. When they are used to their parent coming from a place of empathy rather than control, they respect the seriousness of the request and are less likely to experience it as oppressive. As challenging as it may seem, giving boundaries can be achieved without having to resort to punishments and rewards!

Whether the boundary is set with love, force or a bribe – there will be challenges along the way. By using force or bribes, it may seem to work with compliance in the moment, but how much longer do you think you can do this as the child gets older; when the child turns into a rebellious wild child due to all of the manipulating and apprehensive strategies? Control is not parenting; it doesn't allow the child to gain relationship to the consequences of her choices in the world.

When you are setting boundaries, are they coming from a perspective of support or control? Does the quality (or non-quality) of the relationship outweigh the quick-fix style of parenting? It may seem quicker and easier to just give in or to bribe them so that everyone gets back to being "happy" and you're able to get your needs met; but truthfully, in the bigger picture, it causes disconnect that can bite you in the dairy aire later on.

I recall seeing a friend of mine when my son was around a year old. We wanted to take a picture of my son and his son (about 4 years old at the time) together, but his son didn't want to take the picture. So, of course, the natural thing to do (okay, so it's not necessarily the natural thing, but it's the most common thing that parents do) was to find a way that his son would agree to the picture. And what better way than to get him to do it than by offering a quarter, right? Well, his son decided that a quarter wasn't good enough and wanted 50 cents instead. Talk about a little negotiator! And that's exactly what was being taught: how to negotiate with a sense of "power over" his dad instead of a partnership of "power with."

It may have seemed cute and innocent then, but how much higher will the stakes rise, as he gets older? Fifty cents could turn into an iPad or something even more extravagant.

So why is it that kids continuously test boundaries? Is it normal for them to do this? The answer is yes. As annoying as it may seem, when children are developing, it is actually healthy for children to test their boundaries. They do this not to be manipulative, but to see if the parent is committed to their word. What is helpful when a child is testing the boundary is for the parent to be firm, but gentle, to help guide them in learning how to accept the boundary. Being consistent, adapting the scaffolding to the child's development, and explaining why you are setting the boundary in a clear and positive way, will help the child to understand the intention of the boundary.

Again, it may feel like it takes too long to set a boundary with love and understanding, but the outcome with the quality of your relationship with your child and/or teen as he/she evolves is truly priceless!

Take the time to learn about child development so that you can know at which stage your child is maturing in order to come from an empathetic space when your child's behavior gets unbalanced. While scaffolding, you can actually hold the space for your child to release their upsets and fears around the boundary. What I mean by "holding the space" is giving them the chance to cry, rage and process the boundary, while being loving and gentle, reassuring them that you are there to get them through their feelings, as well as to validate them through the upset.

Here are several suggestions when scaffolding with TLC:

- ***Be Observant*** - Take the time to observe the situation before you assume what is happening. Observe if your child has had her needs met. Has she eaten a nutritious meal, had enough water, taken a nap or had a good rest from the night before? Did she have enough quality time with one adult or were too many hours spent in front of the television or the computer? Did something happen at school? Did they get into a disagreement with their sibling? Has she had a chance to discharge old past hurts or could there be remnants of an earlier emotion that hasn't had a chance to empty out? The list can go on and on so if you can start to do inventory of your child's day to see where the upset might have originated from, more than likely the rest of the frustrations could very well have been a domino effect. Also note that your child could also be dealing with past hurts from a day or even a week ago that they are still trying to process. These are all things to consider when scaffolding. It only takes a few moments to tally whether or not your child has had their cup filled, so that it can help you to also remember this while setting a boundary, in case big feelings arise more than usual. Being observant also entails listening to what your child is saying or doing before you set the boundary.

- **Be Cool and Calm** - When you are able to get down to your child's eye level and approach them with kindness and understanding instead of using harsh words, facial expressions, body language, and/or gestures that intimidate, your child is more receptive to cooperate from a place of openness to you vs. a place in fear of you. Being mindful to how you are energetically setting the boundary is just as important as your tone of voice and facial expressions (as revealed in Chapter Six). As Alfie Kohn states, "the message you send your children is not important. It is the message they receive."

This is not to say that your child won't react to the boundary; but the more you, as the adult, are able to stay in your center (meaning to be present and calm) and communicate empathetically and lovingly, the more the child feels safe to eventually listen. And as challenging as it may be to stay cool and calm, especially when you've got a child who is hitting or kicking, just remember that beneath every aggressive impulse is a deeper, hidden pain that is needing your love and attention. And if you can find it within your heart to remind yourself of this, the easier it will be for you to come back to your center so that you can respond with love instead of react with anger and fear.

- ***Set a Boundary for YOU*** - So often we are focused on scaffolding for our children that perhaps it never occurred to us that sometimes we need a boundary of our own. If you are noticing yourself starting to get triggered, set a healthy boundary for yourself and take a moment for you to get cool and calm again. Tell your child that you are needing a Time Out for yourself to feel more at ease. As a side note, notice nowhere in this book do I suggest a time out for your child because once again that will only create more disconnection and that isn't what this book is about fostering. Once you have set a boundary for yourself, do the next step below.

- ***Stop, Drop, and Pause!*** - Sometimes it's not easy to staying cool and calm. And similar to the oh-so familiar phrase, "Stop, Drop, and Roll", this is a great analogy before you get heated emotionally and need to put your own fire out. It is within the pause that can help us to breathe and re-center. An added benefit is when you start to practice this exercise on a daily basis, it models to your child how they too can self-regulate when flooded with over-heated emotions. And even if your child reacts to the boundary, at least this way, only one of you needs to have their fire tended to.

- ***Be With the Emotions*** - The best thing to do after "Stop, Drop and Pause!" is to be with the sensations. Don't try to dismiss these feelings. But make sure that you don't get stuck in them either. Take a few moments to breathe into your sensations and begin to cool them down. When you find yourself stepping back into authoritarian parenting and starting to criticize, correct, and/or take over by interrupting – "Stop, Drop and Pause!" Allow your breath to bring you back into the present moment. If you have a trusted friend or someone who is a good listener, you can take a few minutes for an emergency offload (away from the earshot of your child). This will allow you to be more present for your child's needs and better aware of your own. Which brings us to the next step.

- ***Be Present*** - Speaking of the present moment, this has been mentioned quite often in this book. So I wanted to share a great way to help when you are too focused on the past or the future and are needing to bring your awareness back into the here and now. I learned this exercise from one of my intuitive mentors. The way you do this is by bringing your thoughts from your head all the way down to the ground. If you think about it, what is the farthest body part from your brain? Yep, your feet! So the concept of this idea is to move your thoughts and ego as far away from your brain. When you start to focus on your feet, it helps to get you out of your head. This is also a wonderful exercise to teach your children, too.

- *Be Real* - The more authentic you are, the more authentic your child can be. Let her know when you're frustrated, sad or disappointed. When you allow her to know that all emotions are valid and it's okay to feel through the emotions without sugarcoating your feelings or going off the deep end with yelling and screaming (which only amounts to scaring them), it opens up the space for them to know their emotions are valid. This also allows your child to connect to your vulnerability; reminding him that you are human and can make mistakes, too.

- *Be Open* - When we open up the discussion on boundary setting with our children, it allows involvement on the child's behalf that helps him to come up with problem-solving ideas and opinions about the boundary. By including him in the discussion of what might work, it can actually gain the child's cooperation in meeting the boundary. Of course, there will be some boundaries that both parties may not agree upon. Some boundaries are just not up for discussion when it involves the child's health and safety. But the more we are open to involving the child in participating in the scaffolding that both the parent and child feel good about, the more we can strengthen the bond. This is especially helpful for teens as they feel that their opinion counts and that you are willing to "work with" as opposed to "doing to".

So what happens if there is disconnection when there is a boundary that has been set? Here's a great example of how I applied scaffolding with love yet firmness that still enabled my son and I to reconnect with cooperation:

I had taken my son to a homeschooling park day. He was around four at the time. The theme for the day was carnival games. And although my son didn't want to play the actual games, children were also receiving tickets when they cheered their fellow peers on during the activities. I was asked to hand out tickets to the kids who were most supportive (not necessarily the loudest, but those who gave the most encouragement).

For the first round of applause, my son was definitely the loudest one that cheered his friends on so I gave him one of the tickets. The next round though I had given to other kids which unfortunately was upsetting to my son who had a melt-down soon after. Yet I could've helped to diffuse the explosive feelings by doing the following:

1. When I received this assignment to hand out tickets, I could've set the stage for my son to let him know what my job was and that I'd be handing out tickets to all the kids who were encouraging their friends.

2. Remember how I mentioned earlier that being observant also entails listening to what your child is saying or doing? Well, after he won the first ticket, and since I was the one in charge of the tickets, my son felt confident enough to state that he was going to be winning another ticket for the next game. Unfortunately, I wasn't being observant and fully present to what he had just said. From his point of view, he might have been thinking that I would naturally give him the next ticket, with me being his mom and all. And when I gave it to another child to be fair, my son felt hurt. When I heard him say that he was going to get another ticket, that could've been my cue to let him know that I'd be giving tickets to all the kids and that maybe he could help me with handing them out.

During the 30 minutes, I used the Time In tool from Chapter Six. I listened as he unleashed his feelings. As he raged and cried and kicked his feet on the grass, I continued to listen. When he would try to kick, hit, and bite me, I would firmly set a boundary by reminding him that hitting hurts, that I wouldn't allow him to hit me and that

I would protect both our bodies. He then proceeded to scream and demand that I give him a ticket. I said very little at this point, as he was in his lower brain and would not understand what words I was saying to him anyway. When he was able to finally calm down, I said, *"You will get a ticket soon but we want to make it fair where everyone else gets a chance to get one too."* The process continued where he was allowed the space to offload his flooded feelings where I reassured him with, *"You are so loved. I'm right here to help you get through your feelings. You're not alone. You're safe with me."*

Lo and behold! After what seemed an eternity, the deeper hurt came out as he cried saying, *"I feel left out!"* So it wasn't so much that I hadn't given him a ticket, it was the fact that he felt left out of the process that he was truly upset about. Again, as mentioned above, if I would've done the above with setting the stage and being more observant with what he had said, I could've invited him to help me pass out the tickets. As we know, when children are able to get their needs met and there is a connection established, they love being our little helpers.

However, I didn't feel guilty or get stuck in the mentality of "should've, would've, or could've." I really appreciated this experience deeply. It not only gave me more practice with Time In, but I was able to stretch myself and feel more comfortable in a public setting where I was surrounded by supportive families. It definitely helped to be in safe environment to practice with a more connected way to scaffold.

So after my son was able to re-regulate himself, we went back to where the children were playing, so that he could continue cheering the kids on. During this time, one of the moms handed my son a ticket. Well, another interesting thing occurred. He took one look at the ticket and noticed that there weren't any pictures on it like the first ticket he received. I could already see the distaste in his eyes as he threw it on the ground.

Now normally by this time, after thirty or so minutes of being patient and working through the big feelings, some parents would've gotten exasperated. Some might have told their child how inappropriate their actions were and how unappreciative they were behaving. Heck, even without the previous incident that occurred, parents would tend to normally react this way. And I have to admit, I almost went there but I knew if I had expressed this even in the most gentle of ways, it would've undone all the hard work that we had done to get re-connected. If I had chosen to go this route, I would have made him feel guilty and wrong, which is not what I wanted to do. Plus, if you really think about it, more than likely he was still expelling the old hurts of the prior explosion.

So I chose to connect instead. I went on to explain, *"There are all kinds of tickets that can look different from each other. Some may have pictures and some don't, but each ticket is useful for something. And when someone gives us something, even if it's a ticket that doesn't have pictures, it's still a gift that we can be grateful for."* Soon after, he cheerfully said, *"Oh. I can even draw a picture on it, too!"* So not only was I able to maintain the connection with my son in that moment, he was able to creatively produce a solution on his own.

It was a lot of patience on my end (something that sometimes we don't always have as parents); but the more we are able to practice patience, the more our children can appreciate and listen when we ask *them* to be patient.

Shortly after that, one of the moms came up to me and shared how impressed she was with how I handled the situation. See that is what it is all about folks! Strengthening the bond with our children while inspiring others to do the same.

Now that we've gone over scaffolding while being cool and calm, the next topic is consequences. There are two different kinds of consequences: natural and coercive. Natural consequences are just that – they occur naturally, while coercive consequences are manipulated by someone enforcing a threat or isolation. For instance, a "time-out" would be a coercive consequence (which we have learned from Chapter Three doesn't work towards connection). Where natural consequences happen without parent involvement or interference, coercive consequences impose punitive tactics that denote punishment. This is where "power over" plays an impending role.

Paraphrased by Alfie Kohn, when dictated by consequences, kids tend to think:

"What do they want me to do, and what will happen to me if I don't do it?"

Whereas when using rewards, kids tend to think, *"What do they want me to do, and what will I get for doing it?"*

These two questions differ from when a child asks, *"What kind of person do I want to be?"* Most children raised with more compassion and mutual respect may tend to ask themselves this question over the other two.

Here are some examples of what can happen when natural or coercive consequences take place:

1. *Child forgets and leaves toys outside in the rain.*

Natural consequence: The toys get rusty and ruined.

Coercive consequence: *"I told you to get your toys from outside and now it's raining! If you don't put your toys away, I won't buy you anymore toys because obviously you don't know how to treat them well!"*

2. *Child refuses to wear his jacket.*

Natural consequence: Child feels cold.

Coercive consequence: *"You never listen to me! How many times have I told you to put your jacket on. You'll catch a cold! If you don't put your jacket on, we're staying home!"*

3. Child forgets to put cat food in the fridge.

> Natural consequence: Cat food gets smelly and can attract ants from outside.
>
> Coercive consequence: *"You forgot to put the cat food away! And now it might attract ants from outside! You're so irresponsible and forgetful!"*

Now although natural consequences do occur, there are other ways to create more cooperation without having to use a coercive consequence. Below are some options for the above situations:

Cooperation Option #1: Describe the situation. When you explain the situation to the child without blaming and shaming, they more than likely will cooperate.

"Your toy cars are outside and it's raining. Because it is metal, it can get rusty."

Cooperation Option #2: Give them choices. By giving your child choices empowers them to more easefully cooperate. Also, being flexible yourself can also alleviate the struggle for cooperation, as well.

"Do you want to wear a sweater or bring your jacket? I need you to have a long sleeve because it's cold outside. If you choose the jacket, we can leave it in the car until you get cold."

Cooperation Option #3: Give Reminders Through Facts. Giving a reminder and information on what you are requesting your child to do rather than yelling and making them feel guilty and wrong can also create more cooperation.

"The cat food is out. If it's out for too long, the ants might come from outside to get to it."

By simply stating the facts, this reminds your child of what needs to be done. It isn't necessary to add in the blame, shame, and guilt.

This only causes more stress between the two of you and if done continuously can strain the relationship altogether as your child gets older.

I'd like to share one more story and how setting boundaries with compassion instead of with an intimidating demeanor has helped my son and how he relates to others in the world. My family was going through a traumatic change. It was during the separation between my husband and me. Not only were we no longer living under the same roof, I had to start working outside of the home (which was my first time having to do so since my son was born). My son's whole world of safety had been swept underneath him. He was four years old. There was a lot of pain and confusion about this and it was being expressed through his play (which is a normal way for our children to expel their feelings and take on different roles as we had discussed in Chapter Six).

During his play dates with one particular friend, when they would get into a disagreement, my son would say some pretty descriptive things that he would do to his friend when he got flooded with feelings that would naturally scare his friend. This was obviously confusing and painful stuff that my son was going through emotionally along with still trying to navigate what these feelings are and what they mean.

Thankfully I have a very understanding friend (Leigh, the same mom whom has six children and practices Quality Parenting). She shared her concerns and because our friendship meant a lot to one another, as well as for our kids – we wanted to find a positive solution where everyone felt heard and safe. So we started "shadowing" the children. Shadowing is when you observe and listen tentatively to your children in close range. This allows the parents to step in to help guide the children when they begin to hear any tension. The point of this is to catch the tension before it boils over into complete flooded feelings where words or actions can cause more distress.

Before arriving for any of our play dates though, I would do these two things with my son: set the stage and set a boundary. This is how the conversation would go:

"So today we are going over to Leigh's to have a play date. It's going to be fun! You get to play together and play with toys that you both feel comfortable sharing. And if either of you start to feel upset during play time, Leigh and I will help you through your big feelings. I also need to set a boundary though so that everyone feels safe and heard. If you start saying those scary words or hit or bite your friend, we will have to leave. I won't be mad. We will just have to leave and maybe you and me can go to the park instead."

It was important that I emphasized the fact that I wasn't mad at him and that it was just about keeping everyone feeling safe. Now if I would've gotten upset with him, punished him, and made him out to be "wrong", we could still be dealing with anger issues with how he communicates to his friends.

It took some time, commitment, and persistence with shadowing until both of us moms felt that my son was able to work through his trauma without using hurtful words or being aggressive. It was completely worth it. And because us parents took the time to voice our concerns compassionately to one another, we were open to finding a positive solution to help our families get through this rough patch. It enabled us adults to model to our children what conscious conflict resolution can look like and it was very powerful!

This is a wonderful example of how when we take the time to practice ways to create that deeper connection with the examples I have shared throughout this book, the results are priceless. I said it before and I will say it again: parenting through connection may seem like it takes longer; but, when you look at the overall picture, it takes just as much time to connect with your child and find strategies that elevate towards empathy, trust, and loving cooperation, as it would if you were to try and find ways to repair the damage that tend to usually follow the use of bribes, coercion, and punishments.

In this chapter, we have discussed coercive consequences, natural consequences, and cooperation options that can help to communicate what you would like for your children to do. Now I would like to share another perspective where parent and child can partner with one another to come up with a solution together without having to set any boundaries or consequences.

This story I'm about to share with you expresses just that. A dear friend of mine, Genesis Ripley and I often have deep conversations of our triumphs and challenges that we experience with our children and how to better support them, ourselves, and our tribe.

Genesis was starting to struggle with having her son get ready in order to leave on time for his baseball practice (which is a passion of his). Every time they would get ready to go, he would be so involved with whatever he was doing that he did not consider helping his mom with preparing to leave. He didn't recognize that his choice was hindering him getting where he needed to be on time, efficiently, and with all of his equipment in hand.

So what Genesis did was help bring things to her son's awareness around her frustration and anxiousness to get him there on time. And she shared her concern (without guilt) with forgetting important equipment that he needed. And because their relationship has always been one of mutual respect, he was able to truly hear all that she shared.

This is such a vital factor in creating a "partnership with" rather than a relationship of "power over". If there is no respect, children won't understand the concept of being respectful because they aren't being modeled what respect looks like towards them.

They started brainstorming ideas to make this situation better. They eventually came up with a solution that they started working into their lives. There were some tweaks here and there but eventually they got to a place that worked for both of them to get out of the house on time. They were able to co-create the solution together with a respectful dialogue where everyone's voice felt heard. Was there a lot of patience on the mom's part? Yes, absolutely. But was it worth it to approach it this way rather than enforcing a consequence, setting a boundary or even a natural consequence? In this situation - yes, absolutely!

Overtime, her son was able to gain a deeper awareness around his choices that were affecting his family, himself, and his team. And overtime, he was able to grow into himself around these areas that allowed him to start choosing on his own – which is instrumental to the model of a partnership of power with that can empower him in all of his relationships.

Just as I had mentioned in Chapter One, another imperative thing that I would like to reiterate over and over again is that children's brains are still developing. So in this situation with my friend's son, most parents might get frustrated thinking that their children are being manipulative, lazy, stubborn, and/or not listening. This is where having a different perspective is essential.

Could it possibly be that the way we perceive our children could be the problem, not their behavior? And yes, perhaps having natural consequences and healthy boundaries are wonderful ways to help guide your children in doing what you want them to do that doesn't entail bullying, blaming, and/or shaming but how remarkable would it be to arrive to a liberated place where the ultimate result is of parenting with mutual respect where your child partners together with you on a solution that supports both of you? Because if you really think about it, natural consequences and setting healthy boundaries still implies somewhat of a relationship of "power over" where our children's decisions come from outside of themselves. Whereas in the example I shared with my friend, her nine-year-old son came up with this solution from within; it was a choice he made based on him seeing how his choices were making his mom feel frustrated and because he was being respected with how she was communicating to him about her frustrations, he was then able to recognize where his choices were playing a part in the frustration.

In retrospect, what if our end goal is to actually reframe the way we are perceiving our children so that we can get to this liberated place where we work together and find solutions through mutual respect and a healthy dialogue? Perhaps it is the distinction with you seeing with a new lens that your child's brain is still developing as opposed to assuming your child is being lazy, malicious, doing something against you, or not wanting to help you. Along with your willingness to see with a new lens and trusting in the process, overtime they will be able to gain a wider view of how their choices affect their families, communities, and the world.

One of my favorite quotes of all time is:

"The real voyage of discovery consists not in seeking new landscapes, but in having new eyes."

— Marcel Proust

I'd also like to point out that it's really not how we use our words either because we can use terminology that is thought to be "conscious" but if we are saying it in an accusatory tone or our body language and facial expressions don't match what these conscious words are trying to portray, the message will still be received as disrespectful and a "power over".

By the way, did I mention already that children's brains are still developing? Ok good! And just as I'm repeating myself, so too that you will find you may have to repeat this process over and over again because of the fact that children's brains are what is that called again? Ah yes – developing!

Now let's go deeper with your own experiences with setting boundaries.

When was a time when you set boundaries with bribes? Did you find it worked? How many times did you have to continue bribing in order to be get your child to cooperate?

Have you ever experienced where you could set boundaries without coercion or bribes? If so, how were you able to set a healthy boundary? How did the new boundary affect your connection? What gift were you able to receive by doing it this way? As a side note, I see every experience (even negative experiences) as an opportunity for growth so when I ask what gift you were you able to receive, what were the positive (or negative) results from taking this approach? What did you notice differently with how your child cooperated or didn't cooperate?

_____
_____
_____

Was there ever a time where your child/teen was able to come up with solutions that were choices from within rather than from a natural consequence or from a boundary? Did the choice stem from a healthy and respectful dialogue around feelings or did it stem from guilt or wanting to do it to "please" you?

_____
_____
_____
_____
_____
_____
_____
_____
_____
_____

Let's rehash what we learned from this chapter. We've learned that scaffolding in a caring and understanding demeanor is important for the child's development. We also discovered eight ways to keep you more at ease when having to set a boundary; and, that there are alternatives to coercive consequences or even setting boundaries that can also establish cooperation, all the while staying connected and calm.

In the upcoming chapter, we will talk about one more step that is probably one of the most important steps on your path to learning more ways to create a deeper connection with your family. Let's turn the page to find out what that is.

Chapter Ten:
What's That Feeling in Your Gut?

*"When you're following what's True for you,
you're allowing those around you to experience what's
True for them."*
~ Amir Zoghi

We all have felt it at one time or another – that feeling within our gut (and I'm not talking about that gassy feeling either)! It's that feeling that tries to tell us when something feels either "right" or "wrong".

When it comes to parenting, I bet there has been at least one experience (if not many) where you intuitively "knew" that something just didn't feel right or felt off with your child. It's as if an internal alarm is going off. Unfortunately, sometimes we second guess the feeling and get so caught up in the heat of the moment that we blindly miss the deeper need.

Sometimes it can be challenging to remain in your center when an older sibling is hitting the baby or when you're getting the silent treatment from your withdrawn child or teen. We forget to tune in to our own knowingness that the hitting is your child expressing his fear and a cry for connection; that the silence coming from your daughter is her muffled fears yearning for connection and approval, too.

When we are in the midst of busy schedules, getting the kids ready for school, preparing meals, doing laundry, working to pay the bills, traveling from activity to activity or trying to get the kids ready for bed, it can sometimes be challenging to listen to that inner voice– especially when there are other voices (i.e. your parents, your parent friends and teachers) that are influencing your decisions.

In the previous chapters, I have given you some wonderful insights from resources that I've learned along the way, including some of my own. But with this particular topic - it's in its own special category. It is something that cannot be seen; it can only be felt. And it is something I cannot tell you exactly how to do, either. I can merely share where the space comes from. And it can be the most rewarding place for you to parent that can guide you on what intuitively feels right for you and your family on your parenting journey.

I will reveal to you a much deeper wisdom within this chapter. I will share:

- What it means to be an intuitive parent

- Where limiting thoughts deter you from the "feeling"

- How to go with the "feeling" and stick with it

So now it's time to go with your feeling and read on, so that you can learn more ways to, well, go with your feeling!

As imperative as it is to learn tools and techniques that create connection, it is also important to flow from your heart. Going with your hunch on what feels true for you and your family is necessary when you want to cultivate a more conscious life style.

I once read from a beautifully written novel, "MidWinter Turns to Spring" by Carnelian Sage, how flamenco guitar playing can echo the same message as intuitive parenting:

> *"Flamenco is not simply about technique or the act of putting your fingers into various positions on the ebony board, or mastering the compás, or the rhythm. And it's not just about learning how to make your fingers fly across the strings. It's about telling a story that flows from here," he said pointing to his heart. "People will forget the way you played your guitar. But a story you tell from here will live on in their hearts forever."*

This struck a chord with me (yes, pun intended) and is very metamorphic to parenting from the heart. Intuitive parenting engages our feelings, as opposed to only thinking of strategies. We can think all day long on what techniques to use best, or whether or not we used it correctly; but if we are not able to blend in our own innate tool within ourselves to feel and choose from that space, then how can we help guide our children to intuitively make decisions that are in their highest good?

When we are able to drop into our feelings more frequently, it is within this space that cliché terms like "being present" and "going with the flow" can truly be acquired.

As mentioned in Chapter Seven, let's touch upon the topic of invalidation again. What invalidating actually does is it teaches children at a young age to not feel and/or to hide their feelings. Thus, as they get older, some may seek ways to numb their feelings through drugs, alcohol, and/or other abusive ways that separate themselves from actually feeling and tapping into their intuition.

So when a child is presented with a dangerous situation, if they have not been guided to go with their feelings and have only been taught to stuff their feelings deep within, it can become more challenging for him/her to sense when something is wrong and doesn't feel right for them. Thus, another reason why validating our children's feelings is essential.

And just as invalidating our emotions is costly to the ability to go with our gut instinct, so, too, can our limiting beliefs play a part in it. We have been conditioned at an early age to have a mind-set of lack.

As Julie Kleinhans (Founder of Youth Empowerment and Education Mentor and Successful Kids Revolution stated:

> *"When we feel that we are not enough (lack) or believe that we do not have enough (lack), or think that others do not support us (lack), then we give off an energetic vibration that says to the universe "I am lack, give me more. I like this because it*

is where I am choosing to focus and therefore what I vibrate at". Now the majority of us are not consciously choosing to vibrate in a place of lack, we've just been programmed to think this way. We've been sold the lie of lack and limitation and bought it lock, stock and barrel!"

The truth of the matter is that the Universe is pregnant with abundance and continues to offer opportunities for us to birth these fruitful experiences into our lives. Fortunately for us, we have the ability to re-program our thoughts, so that we can let go of the limiting beliefs that no longer serve us, in order for new beliefs to be born. The unfortunate part is that because the lack can be so deep-seeded, it can deter us from this Truth. This can blind-sight us into only believing in the limitation vs. feeling into the infinite possibilities that are available to us once we say "Yes!"

I am a firm believer in the word "Yes." When we actually say "Yes" to the feeling and "Yes" to ourselves, it is truly amazing how the Universe supports us in that expression. And how the Universe understands what we are thinking and feeling is directly received through the language of our energy, our vibrations.

And how that vibration is able to bring forth action from you is when you step forward to say, "Yes." I'd like to point out here that saying yes to yourself doesn't mean you have to say yes to everything else, though. You still want to set some boundaries and honor your love cup with how you fill it up. The "Yes" that I'm talking about is when you get a strong sense within, that feels good to you and not something out of obligation or guilt. This is a practice that I learned from one of my mentors I have mentioned before (Amir Zoghi).

But what happens if the "Yes" gets clouded from fears and your own limitations? And where do all these fears stem from, anyway?

Let's say, for instance, there's a man who loves listening to jazz music. Ever since he was a young boy, he was attracted to the melody and how it made him feel. As he would listen to legendary artists, such as Miles Davis and Louis Armstrong scatting and harmonizing to the tempo of trumpets and standup bass riffs, he would begin to feel alive! While growing up, though, he was prohibited from listening to it, because his dad used to call it the "devil's music." And any time he would sneak in some of those sweet rhythms, he would get reprimanded for it. Although he was banned from listening to it, he dreamed of one day becoming a jazz musician and hoped he would be able to get a standup bass of his own. Unfortunately, that dream continued to get crushed as his parent's hard-earned money had to go towards "important" things like putting food on the table or paying bills. The boy was repeatedly told that there's no money in being a musician and he would never amount to anything if he didn't go out and get a "real job." Soon his dreams became silenced, as others' dreams were pushed upon him to become a doctor or a lawyer. So as to receive approval from his family, he went to school to become a lawyer. By doing this, he began living someone else's dream. And just as he was invalidated as a child, he was now starting to invalidate himself as an adult. He was taught to no longer follow his dreams, to no longer follow the feeling of what he loved to do. This continued to show up in his adult life, and whenever he felt called to do something, his thoughts and fears stopped him from pursuing it.

Sound familiar? Maybe this hasn't happened to you personally, but perhaps you have heard of others experiencing this. And, unfortunately, parents tend to push their agendas and expectations onto their children, disregarding what the child is passionate about for the sake of wanting what the parent "thinks" is best for their children; perhaps protecting their child from failure (at least what they consider to be "failure"). Along with parents' agendas, there can be moments where we unconsciously label our children. We label them as shy or emotional or spoiled or having ADHD, etc. And as children grow up, they believe all these stories and labels to be true, only to trickle their beliefs, agenda, expectations, and stories unconsciously onto their children. And so goes the trickle effect.

So when these false beliefs get brought down from generation to generation, it continues to condition and program who a person becomes. Once it is imprinted within one's headspace (what I like to call the Ego Space), the mind can spiral downhill and can begin to question one's capabilities. You start to doubt yourself and the ability to be truly happy. You start asking questions like *"How am I going to be able to afford it?"* or *"What if I'm not good enough?"* or *"How will I find the time to do this?"*

And then the feeling gets buried; the "Yes" turns into a "No" or an impossibility. We are so conditioned from our upbringing with the "coercive consequences" that it filters into the present moment where it can sometimes stifle and withhold us from doing what we love doing. *"If you do this, you won't get that." "If you don't do that, you won't have this."*

Of course, there are natural consequences. For instance, if there isn't a way to create a steady income, we can't pay our bills or put food on the table.

But the "coercive consequences" that I talked about in Chapter Nine are what can cause the fear of the "What If's" and the "How's," which seem to override what we are passionate about doing. This can end up making people bitter, tired and overwhelmed, which can produce frustrated feelings in the place of love that just "gets us by," rather than being truly happy and doing what we love to do.

See, what normally happens is that we feel the feeling (whether it's starting a new career doing what we love, picking up a creative hobby, or trying on a new parenting technique), but then we go into the "story" of *"I can't start a whole new career, because I have to provide for my family, and I'm just too old to try and become a jazz musician"* or *"I just don't have enough time to start knitting"* or *"It is challenging trying to connect with my child; I'm just too tired and all the other parents are going to think I'm too nice and not disciplining my child enough."*

We end up looking to our past, current and future situations and feel it is impossible to do what we love doing; therefore, it blocks us from living the lives that we truly desire. And even when we do say "Yes," the challenge most of the time is that there is a "but" that follows.

"Yes, but..." For example, "Yes, I intuitively feel the desire to do this, but I don't have enough time," or "Yes, I intuitively feel the desire to do that, but I'm broke." So in essence, we are in the constant state of invalidating ourselves and numbing the feeling.

So, what if we were to just go with the feeling? What would happen if we were to erase all the "What If's?" and "How's" and merely go with the feeling of what we love to do? What doors could possibly open up for us?

It goes back to what we were talking about in Chapter Seven about the significance of being validated. When you ensure that your child feels validated and is surrounded with the mindset of abundance, you are truly giving him/her the gift of learning how to go with the feeling and vibrate out into the Universe your call to action.

When you have love for your child and are able to create space, so as to have the capacity to make a whole-hearted decision with what feels right with your parenting philosophy, rather than going into the "story" of how others think you "should" parent, you are manifesting a new story that says parenting through connection is possible. When you have the capacity to follow the feeling of being nurturing, being loving without conditions, being compassionate yet firm with your boundaries and having the capacity to want to connect - then the story morphs to reflect the feeling of becoming a conscious parent.

It all has to begin with us choosing to have the capacity, though. It all begins with a choice, the decision to go with the feeling; to choose to tame the wild child within us parents; to choose to heal from our past traumas and to listen to our hearts to what feels right for our home. Every household and culture is different, so it's what feels resonant for your own family.

All of these tools that I've shared in this book are just some of the ways to create connection within the home. There are many other resources out there that offer avenues to delve into, that help children to grow into confident and loving adults that are resilient yet empathetic towards themselves, others and the planet. And whether you use some or all of the tools from here or out there, it is just as valuable to seek within to ponder on what instinctively feels true for your family. And just as important is allowing your child the choice to feel what is instinctively true for him/her.

Perhaps the quote in the beginning of this chapter makes more sense to you now because when you are following what feels true for you, you are modeling this to your children and to others what can be possible and true for them.

All it takes is for you to choose to shed your old snake skin, to shed your own limiting beliefs, in order to pave a path that not only guides you through loving connection but your children, as well.

So now that we really dove deep into what it means to go with the feeling, to stay with the feeling and why it's fundamental to feel beyond the self-limitations, in this next chapter I will introduce what it takes to help you tame your inner wild child so that you can become more present with your children.

Chapter Eleven:
What is the Secret to Taming Your Inner Wild Child So That Your Buttons Don't Get Pushed (As Much)?

*"Self-love is accepting yourself, as is.
Reach for the stars...but love yourself right where you are."*
~ Unknown

Wow! That quote continues to move me in so many ways, as I am on my own path with loving and accepting who I am, exactly as I am, wherever I am. Not who I was yesterday or who I want to be tomorrow but who I am today - or more so in who I am in every moment. I have to say that loving one's self can definitely be a challenge at times and I am not afraid to admit it, at least not anymore.

Do you remember in the beginning pages, when I stated that this book is not about how to "tame" our children's behavior? And, that it's really about finding ways to tame our thoughts on how our children's behavior is triggering us? It's about digging beyond the behavior and getting to the root cause of why the behavior is out of sorts, for both you and your child.

Have you ever stopped to ponder, *"what is it that my child is doing or feeling that is triggering me to feel upset? And could there be an inner connection of their behavior that is a reflection reminding me of how I was treated as a child?"*

Do you ever feel like you are on autopilot? Does it seem like you're just barely getting by with getting your kids ready, preparing meals and cleaning your household? Not to mention if you have work outside of parenting to do (you know, the work that helps pay the bills)! Seems like we are masters at doing, doing, doing.

And, who are you BEing when all this "doingness" is occurring? How are you treating yourself, your partner/co-partner and/or your children through all this "doingness"? And is your cup full, or is it running on empty?

This portion of the book is probably one of the most significant chapters you will read. In this section, we will ponder on:

- The secret to taming your inner wild child

- Seven steps to help tame your inner wild child

- What it means to fill your own love cup

Of course, we want the best for our children; but more often than not, we are so busy trying to keep the family afloat with all of our responsibilities and activities for the kids that we tend to forget to stop and take a moment to breathe and relax our bodies. We forget to ground ourselves so we can stay fully connected to our children. We forget to take care of our own needs, in order to model to our children that taking care of our own needs is just as important, so that we can be more present in every moment. And while we're forgetting all of these needs, sometimes we forget our own past hurts that haven't yet been healed.

As my late mentor and dear friend, Michelle Barone (whom recently passed away) said:

> *"We all bring to our relationships the good and the bad from our own upbringing. Children will always make us face any unfinished issues we may have from our own childhood. Much of the work I do with parents is helping them to unravel and heal their own childhood hurts so they can bring healthy patterns into their own family."*

Becoming a parent can be the key to unlocking the door to healing the wounded children within us because our children reflect back to us the places within ourselves that need healing whenever we get triggered by a "behavior" that our children are expressing. And when we get triggered and our buttons are being pushed, this is usually due to our own childhood.

In order to heal our wounded self, we must first acknowledge this part of ourselves. Then, we must grow a deeper connection within ourselves by doing things to be more loving to one's self.

I once heard David Byrd, (founder and CEO of David Byrd Consulting, LLC and an inspiring and effective leadership consultant) say:

> *"You can never grow from where you think you should be. You can only grow from where you ARE! The human potential is unlimited. Everyone has a wellspring of unlimited potential that they just haven't tapped into."*

So how can you grow from where you are? It's simple, really. Be what you love to do. Let me repeat that: BE what you love to do. What exactly does that mean? I know...I know it kind of sounds strange murmuring those words from your lips, but let the phrase marinate a little longer. And not in your brain, but within your heart. Trust me, it'll become clear after a while.

In the meantime, let me ask you this question. When you're staring at yourself in the mirror, who else are you loving? Who else are you taking care of? Whose needs are you helping to get met while yours are silently still looking in its reflection...waiting? Waiting for what? Waiting until your children grow up in order for you to do what you love?

As an eco-conscious parenting advocate, I am passionate about becoming more in tune with what will manifest a more conscious world for all of us to live in. Yet before I can fully travel a path of harmonious relations with others, I must manifest a continuum of self-love within me, FOR me first.

And thus is the path for all of us.

A lot of times people tend to do in order to get. But what if the journey isn't about just doing but about *being* in order to receive?

What if all the things that we are doing in the world is only filling up a void in our lives and is stopping us from being in our greatness? OR what if we were to actually do what we truly and passionately love doing (whether through writing, playing music, snowboarding, spending time with your kids or even as simple as drinking your favorite cup of tea - whatever the case may be that you find joy and fulfillment in). How much more could we be for ourselves and for our children when we are actually doing the things we love doing?

I'm sure all of us have heard the phrase, *"In order to be able to love others, you need to be able to fully love yourself."* Well, there is a reason why this phrase buzzes through the atmosphere like a broken record. Most people have yet to accomplish this gift completely.

And, yes, it is a gift. To be able to look in the mirror and truly love your self, without any judgments or expectations, is such a huge aspiration that most of us would like to experience. Isn't it, after all, throughout our whole lives that we have wanted the approval of others, for others to accept us for who we are?

And that's just it – we are constantly looking outside of ourselves for love and happiness and rarely do we start with ourselves first. This form of love is finite; it is with conditions – the conditions for need, acceptance, attachment, expectation, and/or an agenda. The type of conditioning that most of us have experienced from our upbringing. The type of conditioning that tends to repeat itself, just as Michelle Barone's quote above, that most parents continue to model to their children.

It stems from the Ego Space. The Ego tends to derive from a place of need, whereas the Infinite manifests from a space where it absolutely loves to love. In other words, Ego gives love in order to get love back, whereas Infinite love just is...it doesn't need to give or receive it. Unfortunately, people tend to look outside themselves to fill themselves up by "giving" to get love. Going back to Chapter Three, this is the exact conditioning that has been formed from the "Good Job's" that we end up craving as we get older - the approval of others rather than feeling genuinely good from within. We may not even realize it but this even shows up in our online platforms with how many "likes" and "comments" that we tend to crave from our social media "friends".

In the past, I used to find myself in predicaments where I put others before myself. Even before I became a mom, I always thought of others and nurtured their needs before I did mine. And after becoming a mom, well, you can imagine how much more my needs were put on the back burner.

There were days (okay perhaps weeks...alright, months!) that had gone by where I didn't even bat my eyes a wink to realize that I hadn't done something loving for myself. And yes, those days still occur, but not as frequently as before. I had opened up that cricket-y door and cleared the cob-webbed path to my self-love. I started to get in tune with what really quenches my needs with watering my soul with inner connection. And I found it came in the form of meditation, being in nature, writing, dancing, performing or some expression of self-love that allows me to open my heart to my Truth.

This book isn't just about me and my journey. This is yours, as well. So if you're like me and sometimes forget to look in your reflection to smile and kiss yourself, I wanted to give you several tools that can help you in that direction.

So what's the first step to taking care of yourself, you may ask? Do what you love doing! That's it! It's that simple! Yet is it? Unfortunately, we all tend to make it difficult on ourselves - saying we don't have time or we're too tired or too old or too young or too much of this or too little of that!

Fortunately for you, right now in this very moment, you get to choose. Ok, so let's backtrack for a minute here - perhaps the first step is about choice.

So the following are several steps you can take to start getting your needs met. And just so you know, it doesn't have to be in the order listed. There's no right or wrongs about what order you need to take in order to get your needs met; but for the sake of having things be more clear and concise, I've put them in a sequence that will help you to start your journey into loving yourself. Just know, though, that these steps can interchange with one another.

STEP 1. CHOOSE. It's time. It's time to make a decision on whether you will continue making excuses for why you are not doing what you love to do and not taking care of your needs or choose to have a new blank canvas to paint the many colors where you can begin to go with the feeling.

So, before you drive yourself crazy and find yourself spiraling down the rabbit hole, stop! And then choose to feel! When you go with your feeling (back to what we were discussing in Chapter Ten) and trust your intuition, without going into the headspace and the "logical, sensible" reasoning, you will be surprised what doors can open for you when you say "Yes!" to yourself!

STEP 2A. BREATHE. Close your eyes if you feel it will help. Take three deep breaths in and out. Allow the brain chatter to dissipate by focusing on the breath. Feel your breath expanding your diaphragm outward and inward.

Step 2B. BE AWARE. Take it a step further and bring your awareness from your head all the way down to your feet. As mentioned in Chapter Nine, because this is the farthest point from your head, it can help to get you out of your thoughts - which can help you to become more present and grounded.

STEP 3. LISTEN. Once you have chosen to start loving yourself and have slowed down the brain chatter through breathing and focusing your energy on your feet, now it's time to listen; to listen to your heart; actually, let me rephrase, to listen *from* your heart.

Truly take a moment to sit down and think about what drives your passion. Actually don't even think, feel! What does it feel like when you grab for that pen and start ferociously scribbling words on a bar napkin? How does it feel to pick up that guitar and allow your fingers to dance with the strings, to create a rhythm? Or it could even be as simple as sitting on grass and feeling the sun against your face. What would it feel like to actually go with your passions and in return have your needs met?

STEP 4. WRITE. After you've honed in on that feeling, get a piece of paper and write down those things that really make your heart pitter-patter and gets you smiling. Perhaps it's only one item on that list or perhaps it's ten. Perhaps it's meditating, yoga, dancing, journaling, poetry, or drinking tea with a friend. Either way, write it down so you can visually see what it is that you are passionate about. Sure, we may know what gets us ticking and ignites the passion, but writing it down will be a good reminder for you to start doing more of the items on that list.

_____
_____
_____
_____
_____
_____
_____
_____
_____
_____

STEP 5. BE WHAT YOU LOVE TO DO & JUST DO IT! You know the famous Nike saying, *"Just Do It"*? It's a catchy phrase for a reason. Now it's time to look at that piece of paper and start doing what you love to do. I know earlier I had mentioned that people tend to do in order to get. And I had pondered on the question that what if the journey isn't about just doing but about being in order to receive? So perhaps it's not about just doing in order to fill up a void anymore. What is actually possible when we do what we truly love doing that enriches who we are being in the world? What if being what you love to do awakens you to your Truth and fills you up, instead of just filling a void?

Once you are able to come from this space vs. just doing it to do it, you will begin to notice that who you are BEING in the world makes you actually FEEL good about yourself. Thus, you begin to fall in love with the person looking in the mirror, YOU. And simultaneously, you will begin to notice that the world is falling in love with you, too, as opportunities start to present themselves that create abundance in your life. Abundance in happiness, health, financial freedom, and your relationships with your loved ones.

STEP 6. SMILE...A LOT! Whether you're looking at yourself in front of the mirror or walking past a stranger, smile! Research has shown that smiling doesn't only affect one's mood; it can affect one's health, as well. Charles Darwin (the philosopher) and William James (a psychologist) theorized that facial expressions are a main contribution to the actual feeling itself and not just the visible sign of an emotion.

I recently heard an inspiring workshop from Shawn Achor, founder of the Happiness Advantage. His whole concept on happiness is that success isn't a prelude to happiness; that being happy isn't a result of how successful one can be. It is, in fact, just the opposite. It is the feeling of happiness that can make one successful in life!

During his workshop, he shared a great exercise and told the participants to find a partner. Partner B was to do their best to not smile, to remain emotionless and to not even move one inch of their face, while Partner A was to smile immensely for about 60 seconds in order to see if they can get Partner B to break into a smile. Then the partners would switch and do the same thing. The whole object of this exercise was to show when you smile, how the feeling spreads and can affect others around you.

We all know that emotions can tend to be highly contagious, whether it's negative or positive emotions. I'm sure you can attest to this being the truth whenever your child continues to be in a state of frustration, while crying and raging through their feelings, and how it can all of a sudden affect your mood. The same goes for when your child is at peace and in a good mood, and how easily you are able to function empathetically and joyfully.

So whether you're cooking or cleaning or riding in an elevator with a stranger, smile (even if you're having a crummy day, especially when you're having a crummy day)! When you do this, you just might start to feel a lot better about your day, and more importantly, about yourself.

Please note that it's not a "fake it until you make it" attitude either. If you are truly in a state of sadness or anger, allow yourself to feel these emotions by yourself or with a spouse or a friend. Just like you would allow your child to let it out in a healthy way (as mentioned in Chapter Seven), it is also wise to model letting it out yourself (of course, in healthy ways, as well). Just as long as you don't get stuck in that space of feeling sad or angry for too long an amount of time. Feel it and move through it by expressing your emotions through art, dance, writing, music, (as suggested in Chapter Two), meditation, pondering, etc.

Sometimes the mere releasing of our feelings can bring about a smile and shift the energy. By smiling (whether to yourself or to someone else) it can help to elevate you in wanting to continue being in this constant space of feeling love for yourself. And when you are in this constant space of self-love, you start to be who you truly are.

STEP 7. GRATITUDE SHARE. I had mentioned before that in our family we have a tradition right before we eat dinner. After sending loving prayers and intentions into our food, we go around the table to share at least one "Gratitude Share"; something that we are grateful for in the moment. This is a great way to give thanks for all the things in your life.

Being grateful is such an essential piece to the whole puzzle of manifesting what we love to do. When we give thanks, it is vibrating to the Universe that we are ready to manifest more of what we want to attract in our lives. And when we're coming from a space of love and doing what we love to do, we can then come full circle with making choices that provide real happiness - which is definitely something for which to count our blessings.

Here's another great way to share your gratitude:

1. Write down a list of at least five things you are thankful for (the list can be as long as you like, the longer the better)

2. Reflect how the items on the list have made you feel and allow it to be a reminder of how good it felt with each experience, and

3. If there is a person mentioned on the list, then give them a call or send them an email/text to continue the flow of gratitude. In Shawn Achor's "Happiness Advantage" workshop, one of the ways to create more happiness is when you think of one person you are grateful for each day and send them an email or give them a call to let them know just how much you appreciate them.

The goal is to do this for 21 days straight so that you begin a new rhythm that cultivates a new habit. It has been said that it requires 21 days for new neural pathways to be fully formed in the brain. Thus, why it's a good idea to try for 21 days.

In fact, this is actually a useful tool to use when you are frustrated with your child, your spouse, and/or yourself. Write down what you are grateful for with your family members for 21 days and perhaps this could shift how things are at home. This could help to alleviate big feelings about yourself and/or your loved ones. Whether it is more of what you love to do or perhaps more harmony and peace within the home or within yourself that you desire, being grateful can begin to free up the space for you to attract the life you want to live.

STEP 8. GO DEEPER WITH YOUR GRATITUDE. When sharing how grateful you are with your loved ones, go deeper by being specific with a quality that you truly admire about them. Rather than just saying you are thankful for them being in your life, being specific helps both the one giving and the one receiving the gratitude a clearer idea of why you appreciate them which can give them confidence in who they are as a person, all the while bringing you both closer.

Below is an example of a specific way to share your appreciation:

Instead of just saying: *"I'm grateful for you."* You could write: *"I'm grateful for how helpful you are when you _____. It really helps when I need to get dinner on the table and I have noticed that I'm more calm for the rest of the evening when I have some help."*

Recently my business partner, Leigh Sietsema and myself did a 7-Day Gratitude Challenge for our Thread of Connection community that I am now challenging you to go deeper with, too.

1. What specific quality do you appreciate in your child and why? In what ways does this quality bring you joy? How can you be grateful for this quality right now?

    _____
    _____
    _____
    _____
    _____
    _____
    _____
    _____
    _____

2. What traditions/rituals/ceremonies do you do that you are grateful for that brings you joy and creates more connection in your home?

___

3. What specific quality do you appreciate about yourself as a parent? In what way does that grow your relationship with your child? In what way does that make you feel good as a parent?

___

_____
_____
_____
_____
_____

4. What specific quality do you see in your spouse/co-parent that truly shows the connection within your family that you admire and appreciate?

_____
_____
_____
_____
_____
_____
_____
_____
_____
_____
_____
_____
_____
_____
_____

5. List 3 things that are working well in your family that you are grateful for. Again, let's get specific! The more specific you are, the more consciously you can go deeper with the appreciation for the people and the quality of life that you are living and/or want to start living.

6. List 3 things that are challenging (perhaps not working as well as you would like) but are able to see the gift and lesson that it is presenting itself towards you and your family that you can appreciate.

7. Now get out blank paper and write a Gratitude Love Note to your child, to your spouse/coparent/loved one AND one to yourself! Once again please be specific with a quality that you are grateful for. Once you have written these Gratitude Love Notes, give them to your loved ones. The one for you, keep in a place where you can always see it as a reminder of your love for yourself.

When you practice these steps you will soon start to notice that the once "Wild Child" within you can become more tame (calm), more focused and more in alignment with yourself. And when you are connected to yourself, you are more able to be present with connecting with your child.

I truly believe that happiness occurs from the inside out. In order for us to help our children become happy, confident and compassionate beings who are able to move through their emotions and behave in a way that supports their well-being consciously, we, as their chosen guides, must begin with how our own emotions and behaviors are consciously being supported for our well-being.

And what are our emotions and behaviors reflecting back to our children? How are we expressing ourselves (or not expressing ourselves) to them? As challenging as it may be, we must shift our reactions with our children and respond with compassion in order for our children to learn how to respond with compassion, as well. Like I've mentioned many times in this book, we must get past the behavior and find out what the underlying emotion really is. And most importantly we must heal our own past hurts and find ways to connect with ourselves in order to see through a lens of empathy to help our children through their hurts.

So if what we are wanting is to "tame" the wild child behavior within our children, then we must "tame" our point of view of our children's behavior. Therefore, it is important to recognize that there is nothing to tame about our children at all; that it is about supporting and celebrating them in becoming the best versions of themselves while doing the same with supporting and celebrating our best versions of ourselves, as well.

And this isn't to say that you won't ever revert back to old parenting ways, get out of your center or disconnect with your child. We are only human and are capable of making mistakes. Lord knows how many times I have gotten frustrated and disconnected with my son only to turn around quickly to realize what I had done to then apologize and reconnect with him soon after. That is when I become observant and do inventory of where I have gotten off kilter (perhaps where I haven't had enough sleep, or haven't eaten yet or haven't filled up my love cup or perhaps haven't done a combination of these things). Yet the more that you are willing to tame the inner wild child within yourself and choose a path towards conscious parenting with the tools and resources I have shared in this book along with your own innate intuitiveness, the more you can support a relationship within your family that honors mutual respect and compassionate communication.

I wanted to share a heart-inspiring message from Carmine Leo during the interview we did that corresponds to how we relate to our children by healing ourselves first.

> *"One of the essential points of connection parenting, as a parent, we have to do our own inner work. So whatever incompletions that we have with our own childhood and our own experiences of being parented, our kids will find those out right away. Any buttons that we've got that we haven't worked out, they're going to figure it out and nail it. And in truth, in reality - this is one of those messages vs. the messenger. If we can pay attention, we can see that our children are trying to teach us something even if it's unwitting or unconscious."*

In my 365 Days of Conscious Parenting series that I share on Instagram and Facebook, self-love plays such an important role with consciously parenting:

"Conscious parenting is talking to yourself as if you are talking to someone that you love. The way we criticize, judge, and talk to ourselves can affect how we criticize, judge, and talk to our children.

So in order for us to find ways to connect on a more conscious level with our children, we too need to also find ways to connect with our inner child just the same. When we begin to have moments of negative self-talk, it is within these moments to be gentle, to forgive, and to fill up our love cups with what we love doing (i.e. exercise, meditation, journaling, getting out in nature, going for a ride, etc.) that can bring us back to our center. Because our first love and last love is...self-love."

So if you are not experiencing what you love, whether it's your creativity, your expressionism, your passions, then who else are you loving when it's just your reflection in the mirror? Who else is taking up space in your mind and filling it up with their stuff, their issues, their dreams? And are you ready to start fully loving the person that you see in the mirror?

So don't just "try" to do it – decide. It's time to ask yourself, are you ready to decide and choose what you love to do and be who you love being?

One of my favorite mantras from Mahatma Ghandi is: *"Be the change you wish to see in the world."* I'd like to take it a step further and say, *"Be what you love to do and when you're coming from that space, the world will organically transform."*

It's not about changing, fixing or improving who you are; it's about loving who you are being when you are doing what you love to do. And the more that all of us are being what we love to do, the world vibrates at that same level of energy. And that, my friend, is the secret to being able to tame your inner wild child perception of your child's behavior.

Let me ask you this, what if everyone in the world went with the feeling to do what they love doing (without getting stuck in the "what ifs"), wouldn't they then be a full expression of Love? Therefore, it's not necessarily only about "being the change," it is also "being what you love to do" that can transform the world. Yet, it is a choice. It all begins and ends with you and how you choose to live in it.

Please know that this is different from just "doing" by itself. As Amir has quoted: *"You can't do passion or do loving; you can only be passionate and be loving."* So let me just repeat ... the most important step to getting your needs met is to start by being what you love to do!

Because if you aren't doing what you love to do, then who are you being? Would you then just be settling for doing things as a means to an end, a stepping stone that moves you along towards some future reward that sucks all the joy out of it? And, likewise, who are you being when you're coming from a place of settling and not doing what you love to do? Who are you being to yourself? Who are you being to your children? And, just as importantly, in what ways are you role modeling for your children to BE for themselves?

To summarize, in order to be able to love others, you need to be able to fully love yourself. And in order to say "Yes" to ourselves and begin to heal our own wounds, the steps above can help us move through it.

Coming up next, I'll be talking about finding your community because it's not just the child that needs to be raised by a village. You do too!

Chapter Twelve:
Does It Take a Village to Raise a Conscious Parent?

"The best way to find yourself is to lose yourself in the service of others."
~ Mahatma Gandhi

Yes, it truly does take a village to raise a child...er parent. But how can we create a village in today's fast-paced, technological world, where parents are far more isolated from support than ever? And is there such a thing as global community that can really maintain a sense of connectedness for families?

It can get exhausting parenting alone! Most of society has had to take on this lifestyle of either one parent staying home while the other one works or both parents working while the child goes to daycare or school.

It can be a struggle to get everyone's desires met, especially when we feel a sense of isolation from the outside world – a world dominated by parenting methods that aren't aligned with our beliefs. So how can we get the support we need while still maintaining a culture around a more natural, holistic, and connected lifestyle? We can either go find it or build it ourselves.

During this section, you will learn:

- Why community is an integral part of parenting

- Ways to create your own village in order to get support

- Ten values in sustaining a strong foundation within a village

Because I couldn't find any groups in Los Angeles that catered towards a more conscious approach to communicating with children, I decided to start my own community, which you know as FLV. It all began, really, out of the instinctive feeling that there had to be another way to create harmonious and respectful relationships with children.

When our son was born, we lived next door to a woman who had two older kids (around 12 and 17 years old). I heard her constant struggle to connect with her children and what I sensed was her children not feeling heard. Out of a growing frustration at feeling alienated from her children, she resorted to yelling and physical abuse as her only form of communication. As a single mom now, I can relate and empathize to her frustrations of feeling isolated and alone. She struggled to parent from her highest self as she had no tools, resources, or community to support her. From this experience several years ago, a passion awakened within me to build a foundation around conscious parenting and conscious community. There had to be another way to foster relationships with the younger generation–

one that nurtures their experience vs. stifling it.

That's when I discovered the book by Pam Leo. This was the book that gave me hope that there truly was something out there with tools to actively create what I had been yearning for. The absolute beauty of when you are manifesting your own village is that suddenly more doors open up to other like-minded communities. And, as you have read within these pages, I have gratefully discovered more conscious parenting mentors, tools and resources that all generate connection. But it was this first book that brought me down a path that I had no idea would become what it is today – my life's work, my ambition and the reason community is so important to me.

It all began with four families who got together to read this book and discuss the concepts, as well as weave its philosophy into our lives. Soon after the intensive book club was over, we decided that we wanted to continue supporting one another. More families got wind of our group and wanted to join. What started out as a small gathering to explore this book expanded as the vision grew and continued to evolve…a vision to connect families, support and educate ourselves with a gently guided approach to communicating with our children, as well as to learn about holistic wellness and how to connect with and nurture our planet. Thus, Family Love Village (FLV) was born.

So why is community so important?

Community is important because it brings people together. Community is about supporting and relating to one another in a positive way with a common interest. Whether it's a common, vested interest in the well-being of a small group or it expands to the well-being on a vast global standpoint, it is necessary because it builds relationships, generates trust, and keeps us all connected. These are fundamental seedlings required in cultivating a tribe that thrives. A thriving community is like an organic garden; it must be nourished with the purest of nutrients and love in order for it to grow. And when it comes to raising our children in a conscious and unconditionally loving environment (yes, it can be done), the question is whether we want to find other like-minded families to nurture that connection or to do it alone?

How about global community… Can community exist in cyber space?

Within the past few decades, technology has advanced so much that, yes, creating a "global village" is possible. Forums, boards, Facebook groups, Skype, video…the list goes on with how we can grow our community. All of these have been wonderful ways to support one another via the Internet. It continues to allow people to live and connect on a global scale. Through the medium of the Internet, we can form completely new sociological cultures, transforming cultural perspectives of our lives.

Within the rumblings of Mama Gaia, within the yearning of our hearts, there has been a stillness that has been patiently waiting for its magic to re-appear, to re-awaken. And within the awakening, an essential element in harvesting this magic is within intentional relationships. It is time. It is time to reverberate our conscious parenting culture as one collective voice so that it echoes into the Universe where we can touch the lives of many.

Consciously parenting is challenging; and, for many generations, there were very few or no resources and tools on how to become an unconditionally loving parent. Our parents and grandparents only knew what they knew. But now we have wonderful resources such as Pam Leo, Alfie Kohn, Ruth Beaglehole to name a few. We've got books, we've got DVDs, we've got tele-seminars, and we've got the Internet. So the time is now to come together and bring awareness to families and caregivers about these tools and resources. I read an awesome phrase not too long ago… *"we're not just raising children here, we're raising adults."*

Yes, children are our future. But it is within the present moment where positive transformation needs to occur in order for us to give birth to a future that thrives. It is the "survival of the fittest" old way of thinking that has stumped our growth. We need a conscious collective to shift us into a new thought – one that evolves us towards uniting all living things.

Yes it truly does take a village to raise a child. But it also takes a conscious community to give support to conscious parents. Unfortunately in our modern society, most families don't get that opportunity to have many members of a village to get that support. Raising a child can have its challenges - add siblings or other family members to care for (let alone getting our desires and wants fulfilled), and it can get a little overwhelming. Actually, a lot overwhelming, as I'm sure most parents will agree. So this is why it is crucial to find your village, wherever you are. Even if you live in a rural area, you can still find your tribe online. It may not be the same as actually having your tribe in person, but to at least know that you have some form of support from other like-minded families, even on the World Wide Web, can still be helpful.

A big part of feeling supported is being able to release our own big feelings with another compassionate and conscious adult. When we are able to talk to a friend who holds the space for us to expel all of our own hurts and frustrations, it can relieve the way we respond to our children when they are hurting and/or frustrated.

Talking to a friend over the phone or getting together for a cup of tea to vent and let it out is helpful. An even more helpful way to let it out is through a structured technique called Listening Partnership from Hand in Hand Parenting. This is where both parties are in agreement to take turns with a set time for listening. While one is talking, the other is actively listening, without giving advice or interrupting. And then, when the other person's turn is up, the one who spoke becomes the listener.

The concept of this is to release your thoughts, feelings and frustrations without it becoming a "bitching" session. By keeping it as neutral as possible, it lets the parent refrain from getting "stuck in the story" and able to even find solutions within themselves just by letting out their experience. It actually becomes more productive in helping you to heal from your frustrations and fears that can accompany parenting.

Following are some actions that create community:

- ***Giving It Forward*** - Family Love Village (FLV) has a program called Ubuntu where we weave in the essence of a common saying we derived from the same word that is fundamental within the African culture and means to have human kindness and compassion. We do this by volunteering time for organizing meal deliveries for new families or injured families, swapping childcare, gardening, cleaning, or whatever needs that may arise for families where they could use a helping hand. So this is definitely something that can help create more connection and support.

   Speaking of swapping childcare, Jessica Maria Hicks gave a great example when she spoke for FLV on how parents can get their needs met and create community. Moms and dads can do a trade with watching the kids, while the other mom and dad go on a date or get errands done. Perhaps four parents commit to setting a date twice a week, and two of the parents watch all the kids on a set day while the other parents do errands. Then the first set of parents does their errands on another set date, while the other two parents watch the kids. This could be done with moms and dads or with four moms or four dads. The point is that twice a week, your kids are having play dates and peer interaction, and once a week you're hanging out and doing what you'd be doing, anyway, with a friend. This has been a godsend within my homeschooling community and has been vital for me and my son getting our needs met with me having to work and my son needing play dates.

- ***Communal Service*** - One of FLV's other programs is called "Play dates 4 a Cause," where we coordinate outings to serve the greater community with our children. This allows us to give back to the community and give to our children the experience of conscious living and compassion. Play date examples include: visiting a farm for rescued animals, cleaning up the beach and donating items such as clothes, books, and toys to families in need.

- ***Communal Art*** - Another one of our programs is called EAKK! (which stands for EcoArt Kidz Kollectiv!). This is an eco-interactive environment for children and parents to discover and learn the value of creating fun and educational art projects from recycled materials. We bring this program to festivals and events to not only create art from junk, but to also educate on how to become more eco-friendly and having less in the landfills and oceans.

Finding similar programs or even creating your own in your city is a wonderful way to build community.

Along with ways to build support around community, here is a list of ways that can strengthen your tribe, as well.

10 Ways To Cultivate a Thriving Community

1. ***Culture*** – In order to build a thriving community, it is important to instill a common thread of inherent ideas, beliefs, and values that bonds people together.

2. ***Diversity*** – When we welcome all races, ages, genders, ethnicities, sexual orientations, abilities and disabilities into a community, we help its foundation blossom by celebrating our differences, and at the same time honoring its culture's overall vision.

3. ***Transparency and Trust*** – When a community is open, genuine, and upfront - without a hidden agenda, people can begin to trust in one another. When these values are rooted within its culture without judgment, its members become pillars of support.

4. ***Inclusion and Acceptance*** – When we co-create a sacred place where everyone is included and our voices matter - a space where we are rejoiced and accepted as who we are, without being judged; and when we are embraced regardless of where we are in our parenting journey - these are what empower a community.

5. ***Willingness*** – When we are given the freedom to be who we are, we naturally open up to the willingness to learn and grow as a village, leading to a state of symbiosis.

6. ***Engagement and Participation*** – When we encourage connection and a sense of a shared purpose, conversations and actions awaken something greater than ourselves - a feeling that anything can be achieved together. Joining in and collaborating with on-going projects to make a difference (e.g.. workshops with conscious speakers, beach cleanups, a community garden, engaging on Internet forums, helping one another in need, etc.) help a community to flourish.

7. ***Encouragement*** – A thriving community is only as strong as its people. When we take the time to reach out to everyone - being

supportive and encouraging to one another on our parenting path, this becomes the glue that holds the foundation together.

8. *Ability to Listen* – It goes back to the concept that when people feel heard, they begin to heal. Practicing empathetic listening should be encouraged within the community. Listening to each other's challenges, disappointments, and triumphs, as well as to what is working and not working for the community as a whole, is a key factor in the evolvement of the group.

9. *Acknowledgment and Appreciation* – Truly acknowledging one another, and being appreciative of everyone's accomplishments regardless of where they are in their parenting journey, is vital.

10. *Celebration* – A beautiful part of the conscious parenting journey and the building of a tribe with others, is celebrating each other's gifts, skills, and strengths. Doing so, helps each person individually, as well as collectively.

When people are supported by a flourishing community, they are able to birth, parent, and live with presence, connection, and balance. Conscious parenting can begin way before the actual birth. And when parents feel well supported during the pregnancy and birthing process, they will create a strong connection to their inner wisdom and continue to parent in ease-filled, joyful ways with their child.

Parenting may not always be easy; but when we have a support system in place on a regular basis, it can make such a difference for us and for our children. It is, after all, our children who will raise the next generation. So it goes back to the question of whether we want to do conscious parenting alone, or would we rather be part of a community that fosters our innate desire to connect? When we have unconditional connection to community, nature, and ourselves, it is within these elements that we are able to get our needs met in order for our children to get their needs met, as well.

EPILOGUE

In the end, it's really not about our children's behavior that requires changing or "taming." As parents, it is our own behavior that we need to reflect upon in order for us to consciously raise our children! It is our parents' parenting philosophies that are being recycled into our own philosophy. And it is the voices in our own heads (the insecurities and fears that were embedded in us from our upbringing) that need taming. Sure, we may have some filters and may feel it isn't as bad as what we grew up in, but it is still recycled patterns. So if you think about it, in order for us to create a deeper connection that encourages confidence and kindness with our children, it is not our children we need to tame but our own habitual behaviors; our own past experiences that are making us feel uncomfortable whenever our children "behave" in "unacceptable" ways (because perhaps it was not accepted by our parents and their parents and so on). It is the recycled parenting patterns that need nourishing, in order for us to refrain from disconnecting with our children.

Once we are able to do this, the parent/child dynamic completely transforms. Not to say that there won't be disconnection and hiccups along the way, but at least there is now a roadmap to help guide your family towards a more harmonious, mutually respectful journey that, believe it or not, can lead to non-judgmental and truly unconditional love.

And again, there is no strict "right" or "wrong" way to consciously parent your child when connection is the main goal. It is whatever is feeling true for your family. As mentioned, these are merely guidelines and tools that have worked in my experience; and I have been a witness to seeing it work for other families in creating connection. I'd like to also point out that parenting through connection isn't just about acquiring tools to use, it is a way of life; a philosophy.

This philosophy does require patience, but it is so worth it in the long run. I'll repeat it here again – parenting through connection may seem like it takes longer; but when you look at the overall picture - with bribes, coercion and punishments - we are just putting a band-aide on repeat behavior, instead of tending to the gaping wound the child is trying to express. Therefore, it would take just as much time to connect with your child and find strategies that elevate towards empathy, trust, and loving cooperation, as it would if you were to try and find ways to repair the damage that tends to follow the use of bribes, coercion, and punishments.

We can either choose to be trailblazers, who lead a path through connection that empowers our children, or we can bring them down a road that can eventually dim their light. In order for our children to truly become emotionally and socially healthy out in the "real world," the spark needs to be ignited within the home first. And it will be through our choices of how we want to create that connection with our children that matters. As mentioned in a prior chapter, we aren't just raising children; we're ultimately raising adults. And if we all want to raise confident, compassionate and resilient adults, then it must start with how we are guiding and modeling that to our children now.

There are two main choices that can determine the outcome of whether you and your child are connected or not. And it stems from whether you are reacting from a place of fear that usually tends to lead to words and actions that create disconnection, or a place of love, where the response allows you to feel confident, compassionate and more connected to yourself and your family.

Love is universal. It is the one most powerful feeling that, when expressed, can drastically improve a polluted lake into a thriving body of water. Back in the 1990's, Dr. Masaru Emoto conducted an experiment that changed the structural formation of ice crystals. The overall concept is when love, positive thoughts, meditation, prayer, and healing music influence certain water structures, it can completely transform water. Where fear can destroy a whole water supply, love can re-structure it tenfold.

To go even deeper, the average human body is anywhere from 50-80% water. So if you really think about it, if our thoughts and feelings can change the molecular structure of water within the lake, how much more can thoughts and feelings affect our human bodies?

So the question lies within – are you willing to give space and send love to the molecular structure of your thoughts in order to tame the wild child inside yourself, so you can be more available and more present for your child? Are you willing to fill your own love cup, so you can be a container for your child to fill theirs...to take the baby steps mentioned in this book that can strengthen the bond for your family, and be willing to give up the quick-fix parenting for a healthier, happier, and longer-lasting relationship with your child?

The question to ask yourself is would you prefer co-creating a lasting relationship with your children that lasts a lifetime or do you just want to tolerate them until they are 18 years old and can move out? Before you answer that question, quiet your mind and open your heart - which of these two choices would you really, truly prefer?

Because not only is love universal, it is also a universal language. And conscious connection is the translator to a healthy, happy, and loving home. Each household, each village, each culture, each rhythm are extensions of each other...we are just unique dialects of the same mother tongue.

And please remember, it's not about shaming or blaming or making you feel guilty about your prior choices. As a matter of fact, it's not at all about shaming or blaming or making you feel guilty about yourself. Conscious parenting is not about getting it perfect! The fact that it is imperfect is actually perfection in itself because you get to choose in every moment to learn and grow (and it doesn't stop when our kids leave the house, either). . .

And I know all of what you have been reading within these pages may not come easy! Coming from my own experience of being a single, co-parenting mom, there were many times where I felt like throwing my hands up in the air in dire straits. The tears I have cried at night when my son was asleep or even in the midst of frustration when I'm not able to "Stop, Drop, and Pause!" - and have gotten upset and yelled. It was about forgiving myself, being gentle with the innocent, little girl inside of me and knowing the triggers that my son was displaying had nothing, absolutely nothing to do with him but had everything to do with the places inside of me where I needed healing. And it has usually stemmed from somewhere along the way on my own personal journey growing up where I didn't feel acknowledged, accepted, approved of, and loved.

Again, it's not always easy choosing this path with parenting through connection. There have definitely been bumps and detours along the way. I'm only human after all – just like all of you reading this book here with me. Triggers will come up but just know these triggers are not about your children; it is a missing piece/void within yourself from your childhood that is provoking a memory where you possibly didn't feel heard, accepted, appreciated, and acknowledged. But when we continue to have the courage to move towards co-creating a lasting relationship with our children that instills mutual respect, compassion, and empathy - trust me, it is so damn worth it!

It is a journey towards…it is not the end place. So be gentle to yourself along the way. And know that it may take time to tame your inner wild child with the destructive voices in your head. And most importantly, it is about being a positive role model of self-love to your children by being brave enough to connect to your own inner wounded child, while at the same time getting your needs met so that you can re-connect with the child you are raising.

So now you have awareness of the wild child within yourself. You have learned that the "buttons" children press might actually be a gift for you to revisit some of the ghosts from your own past and childhood. You have gained a few more tools for connection and have learned a new philosophy that creates a deeper connection with your children and yourself. You can now take a new path to step forward into your own intuition. The choice is truly yours to embrace.

As I once was told, *"the only thing in the way of who you truly are is one thought."* It only takes one thought to either bog you down or uplift you. One thought to create connection or disconnection within your family. One thought to create connection or disconnection within yourself. You are only one thought away from being a prisoner in your own mind or manifestor of your own reality.

The question is, what will the thought be that will lead to a choice in living your Truth? And even more importantly, what *feeling* will you follow so you are able to guide your children in living theirs?

IT TRULY DOES TAKE A VILLAGE
ACKNOWLEDGEMENTS

There are so many amazing people I would like to thank, who have supported me along the way.

To my son, Andrik, who is my greatest teacher and inspiration for this book. You allow me the opportunity to continuously be in the practice of patience, empathy and, most importantly, how to live in and embrace the present moment. Thank you for choosing me as your guide in life. You have a way of lighting up a room and bringing it to life with your vibrant energy! You have a special gift with bringing out the fun and laughter in others. Thank you for bringing the inner child within me alive!

To Dalmacio Pueblos – Thank you for being such an integral part of our son's life and for continuing to do this dance with me that is called co-parenting. I am in deep gratitude to you and our ever-evolving relationship to one another in helping to raise our son together. The amount of love and commitment you have for our son is priceless! No amount of money or gifts can replace the gift of presence that you so mindfully give to our son. Thank you from the depths of my heart.

To my mom, Dotti Yells, who has been my role model ever since that fateful night when we were able to release old past hurts and begin connecting in an unconditionally loving space. A huge thanks for being the tech-savvy mom that you are, who has helped build my website and newsletter and has been my go-to for any technical issues. Thank you for being the Village Nana (aka DotMom) for Family Love Village and caring for all of our children. Not only has your technical skills with building my businesses and watching over our children been extremely helpful, but the way you exude what the true meaning of what unconditional love is to everything and everyone around you is what I aspire to be.

To my beautiful Sees and best friend, Vivi Angelica Veloso – your never-ending commitment to family always coming first continues to inspire me and warms my heart. Thank you for always being here for me. Through thick and thin, you have always been such a beautiful reflection of light in my life. A continuous sounding board on our spiritual path together – thank you for always sharing your light in this way. Thank you Sees for being my number 1 supporter who always has my back!

To my dad, Robert Veloso - thank you for always taking me on a spiritual journey that continues to deepen my experience. Your commitment in sharing your wisdom and bringing other tools to enlighten my journey has continued to allow me to listen to my inner guidance. I also want to express my deepest gratitude for all of your amazing financial support and guidance with getting this book out to the masses. Thank you for continuously supporting me in all my passions!

To my step-mom, Tutti Veloso - thank you for the continuous support that you have given me throughout the writing of my book. Your vast knowledge with your own writing and publishing expertise, as well as your spiritual insights, has been completely supportive throughout this book and throughout my life. Thank you for being such an inspiration in my life.

To Papa Rick and Danielle for being such an essential part of me and Andrik's lives. Witnessing my son's eyes light up every time he hears your voice, Papa or sees you tickles me pink with joy. Danielle – I see the beauty within you continuing to shine and evolve. Thank you for being you and for being my beautiful Sees!!

To Cindy Avila, otherwise known as Ninny – the world's best nanny and sought after caregiver in the conscious parenting/ homeschooling community! I knew there was something extra special about you when I asked if you would be willing to read a couple of conscious parenting books before your first day on the job. You didn't even hesitate! Your insatiable desire to soak in as many conscious parenting resources in order to create deeper connections with children and their families is priceless. Thank you from the bottom of my heart for all that you have done for my family and so many other families.

To all of my family members (which I can't name here because well, for those that are familiar with the Filipino culture, there are just too many of us to mention) – thank you for being the most talented, hilarious, loving, forgiving and amazing group of Filipinos (or as my mom calls us, EurAsians) I know! I am honored to be from a lineage of empowering activists, healers, artists, performers, comedians, and lovers of life!

To the board members, coordinators, original veterans: Sonia Wike, Eva Lea, Jennifer Kelly, Crystal D'Angora, Sean Wike, Travis Lea, Cory Park, Raul Leckie, Ariel and Otelia Vergez, Lauren Tucker, and all the families that have been the pillars of support for one another and to Family Love Village (FLV) - thank you for having that same innate desire to find our tribe and for believing in the vision of FLV. To Sonia and Eva - the magic behind our trio spearheading - all bundled into one! Thank you for your amazing and diligent work and commitment with producing our EAKK! (EcoArt Kidz Kollectiv!) program together that we bring to music and art festivals. We have been through thick and thin together and I cannot imagine going on this journey without either of you two sisters in my life! To ALL of our FLVolunteers that are so completely dedicated in co-creating a safe, sacred, and fun space for families at these festivals (you know who you are) - a HUGE shout out goes to you all! To Crystal for your beautiful commitment in our Playdates 4 a Cause program where we initiate and coordinate compassionate activities and events for families and to Jennifer for always hosting and helping to organize our local FLV conscious parenting/conscious living workshops and gatherings. Thank you for the beautiful sisterhood and brotherhood we have all co-created together. Without all of you, FLV wouldn't be what it is today. Thank you from the bottom of my heart.

To my dear friend and partner for A Thread of Connection, (another wonderful conscious community which focuses on mutual respect and authentic communication for the whole family) Leigh Sietsema

– I am truly grateful and honored to be walking on this empowering path together, as we pave the way towards our conscious parenting vision and movement. Thank you to you and your family for being such an inspiration and modeling what mutual respect and authentic communication can truly look like. You have created a village within your own home with your six children and supportive husband that I truly admire; a family that I am honored to get the opportunity to be a part of with my son!

To my soul sister, Genesis Ripley – for your constant unconditional support and our deep conversations where we continue to enrich each other and our families' lives. Thank you for your poetic insight as my sounding board throughout the pages of this book. Your eloquent expression is something I will forever remember and appreciate. And a big thank you to your son for putting up with us working hours on end that one night, too!

To our homeschooling community, Genesis Ripley, Jackie Duarte and Damali Navarro. The way you and your families continue to show up for my son and me is a gift of what a village truly is meant to be. When I needed to work, you mamas created the space for our homeschooling families to be together in order for my son and me to get our needs met at the same time. No amount of words can express what my heart continues to feel for those moments when I truly needed support and community. Thank you for this.

To Kim Somers-Egelsee – it has been an honor learning and being certified by you through your Ten Plus Confidence Life Coaching program. Thank you for intuitively seeing in me my true purpose in becoming a conscious co-parenting life coach. Your wisdom as a life coach, speaker, beacon of inspiration through your masterminds and a dear friend has been precious gifts that I will always be deeply appreciative towards.

For Susie Augustin – your enlightening expertise as an author and publisher has been extremely invaluable for me. Having the opportunity to learn from you has re-sparked my first love and passion for writing. Truly in deep gratitude to you!

If it weren't for these two experts mentioned above encouraging me in their Speaking and Writing to Wow mastermind, I wouldn't be where I am today with the revision of this book. So a HUGE thank you to the both of you Kim and Susie for being the catalyst and for believing in me.

To Tiffany Avans – the most amazing editor ever! No amount of words can fully express my deepest gratitude for all that you have done to help me get my book edited. The long nights and calls back and forth to ensure everything was ready to print, thank you my new friend!

To all my mentors (there are too many to mention here, but their wisdom is sprinkled throughout the book) – I'm in such deep gratitude to all of you for being the pioneers in conscious parenting and conscious living that has paved the way for all parents seeking another way to connect and create harmony within their own homes.

Thank you all for playing such an important role in my life so that I can continue to evolve from a heart-centered space.

INDEX

Affection – 11, 54

Attachment parenting – 18, 53-55, 71, 76, 100, 175

Authoritarian parenting – 26-27, 38-39, 49, 53, 66, 134, 141

Autonomy - 33

Big feelings – 6, 8, 45, 49, 74, 78, 85, 93, 96-97, 113, 119, 139, 146, 152, 183, 200

Boundary – 34, 88, 95, 106, 136, 141, 143, 145, 151, 158

Bribes – 25, 27-28, 43, 45-47, 134, 137, 153, 157

Bully/Bullying – 11, 13, 65-66, 68, 106, 107, 155

Child-led – 76, 91, 94-95, 110

Coercion – 27-28, 45, 47, 85, 134, 153, 157

Coercive consequence – 147-150, 153, 159, 167

Community – 38, 57, 72, 76, 130, 184, 194, 205

Compassion – 6, 8, 20, 37, 42, 52, 54, 71, 76-77, 108, 114-115, 121, 127, 130, 134, 136, 148, 150, 152, 168, 189-191, 200-202

Conditional parenting – 30, 40

Connection parenting – 69-70, 100, 191

Conscious parenting – 55, 73-76, 78-79, 83, 96, 113, 134, 169, 190-191, 195-197, 199, 204-205

Cooperation – 20, 47, 54, 71, 94, 124, 143, 149-150, 153, 159

Discipline – 27, 30

Emotional Intelligence – 2, 8-9, 69, 100

Empathy – 8, 20, 47, 49, 54, 70, 72, 127, 131, 134, 136, 153, 190

Empower – 31, 38, 47, 149, 155, 163

Environment – 4, 12, 18-19, 53-54, 79, 99, 118, 133, 146, 198, 202

Family Love Village – 65, 69, 70, 76, 90, 100, 197, 201

Gratitude – 100, 122, 182-184, 189

    Gratitude Love Notes - 189

Healthy boundary/boundaries – 39, 88, 95, 135-136, 141, 155, 157

Intuition – 163, 178

Isolation – 6, 29-30, 49, 84, 147, 195-196

Invalidation – 28, 99, 100-101, 106, 108-109, 134, 163, 165, 167

Natural consequence – 135, 147-149, 153-155, 158, 167

Non-violent communication - 77

Permissive parenting – 27, 38-39, 49, 53, 134-135

Playlistening – 88, 91, 94-95, 97, 111-112, 124

Power/Power Over/Power Struggle – 27, 39, 46, 72, 75, 92-93, 124, 138, 148, 154-156

Quality parenting – 106, 108, 151

Quick fix parenting – 26, 56, 69

Recycled parenting patterns – 26, 84, 132

Reflective Listening – 87

Respect – 19, 28, 33, 37, 44, 53, 55, 74, 77, 115, 117, 132, 136, 148, 154-156, 158, 191, 196

Rites of passage – 118, 128-130

Scaffolding – 135-136, 138-140, 143, 146-147, 159

Self-love – 25, 79, 130, 171, 174, 176, 182, 191-192

Set the stage – 87, 97, 122-124, 132, 144-145, 151

Special Time – 94-97, 122

Stop, Drop, and Pause! - 141

Time In – 12, 45, 84-85, 87-88, 93-94, 97, 145-146

Trauma – 9, 24, 26-27, 81, 120-121, 150, 152, 169

Triad of Connection – 82-84, 88, 94

Validation – 98-99, 107, 109, 111, 114-115, 139, 163, 168

Village – 195, 200, 204

REFERENCES

1. Gary M. Radke, (2005)

2. Vail, P. Emotion: The On/Off Switch for Learning. Modern Learning Press. New York: 1994. Print.

3. Zoghi, A. (2011, quoted in Truth of the Day. Book 1, by Amir Zoghi and the Universe, 2011)

4. J. Kelly. Personal communication, April 17, 2013.

5. Bachner, E. Personal Communication. November 2009.

6. C. Morasky. Personal communication. March 20, 2013.

7. Nerburn, K. Letters to My Son. New World Library. Novato: 1999. Print. Website: http://kentnerburn.com

8. Dale, C. Personal Communication. December, 18, 2010.

9. R. Beaglehole. Personal communication. March 9, 2011.

10. Einstein, A. (October 26, 1929). The Saturday Evening Post, What Life Means to Einstein: An Interview by George Sylvester Viereck, Start Page 17, Quote Page 117, Column 1, Saturday Evening Post Society, Indianapolis, Indiana.

11. Wipfler, P. (n.d.). Citing Websites. In "It's Mine!" All About Sharing. Retrieved June 13, 2013 from http://www.handinhandparenting.org/news/6/64/It-s-Mine-All- About-Sharing

12. Leo, P. (n.d.). Citing Websites. In Connection Parenting and Optimal Child Development. Retrieved June 3, 2013, from http://connectionparenting.com

13. Millman, Dan. The Way of the Peaceful Warrior. HJ Kramer. Novato: 1980. Print.

14. Benet, L. LA ePub Workshop. February 1, 2013. Website: http://www.larrybenet.com

15. Olson, J. The Slight Edge. Success Books. Texas: 2005, 2011. Print.

16. Sears, W. (n.d.). Citing Websites. In Ask Dr. Sears. Retrieved June 3, 2013, from http://www.askdrsears.com/topics/attachment-parenting

17. Center for Science in the Public Interest. Citing Websites. In CSPI Newsroom. Retrieved March 7, 2013, from http://cspinet.org/new/adhdpr.html

18. Campbell, T. (June 11, 2011). Citing Websites. In Can Neuro Emotional Technique (NET), Chiropractic Healing and Nutrition Influence You and Your Family's Overall Health? Retrieved September 20, 2012, from http://

familylovevillage.com/2012/09/how-to-live-in-optimal-health-12-tips-that-can-support-your-immune-system/

19. Wike, S. Personal communication. January 10, 2011

20. Leo, C. Personal communication. April 24, 2013

21. Leo, P. (n.d.). Citing Websites. In Connection Parenting and Optimal Child Development. Retrieved June 3, 2013, from http://connectionparenting.com

22. Olson, J. The Slight Edge. Success Books. Texas: 2005, 2011. Print.

23. Huxley, A. The Art of Seeing. Creative Arts Book Company. 1982. Print.

24. Rosenberg, M. (n.d.). Citing Websites. In Nonviolent Communication. Retrieved June 5, 2013, from http://www.nonviolentcommunication.com/index.htm

25. Beaglehole, R. (n.d.). Citing Websites. In Philosophy Practices. Retrieved June 12, 2012, from http://www.echoparenting.org/who-we-are/philosophy-practices

26. Zoghi, A. (2011, quoted in Truth of the Day. Book 1, by Amir Zoghi and the Universe, 2011)

27. Richards, E. (n.d.). Citing Websites. In Famous Silence Quotes. Retrieved April 7, 2013, from http://www.findquotes.com/tquotes-Silence/3.html

28. Idleman, J. (n.d.). Citing Websites. In Parent Education: Staylistening. Retrieved June 1, 2013, from http://www.handinhandparenting.org/news/175/64/Parent-Education---Staylistening

29. Gordon, K. (March 16, 2013). Citing Websites. In FLV Presents: "Stop Blowing Your Top: How to Stay Calm & Unconditionally Connected to Your Kids - No Matter What!" Retrieved June 3, 2013, from https://www.facebook.com/groups/familylovevillage/

30. Leo, P. (n.d.). Citing Websites. In Natural Child. Retrieved June 3, 2013, from http://www.naturalchild.org/pam_leo/love_cup.html

31. Wipfler, P. (n.d.). Citing Websites. In Playlistening. Retrieved June 1, 2013, from http://www.handinhandparenting.org/news/56/64/Playlistening

32. Kohn, A. The Homework Myth: Why Our Kids Get Too Much of a Bad Thing. Da Capo Press. Cambridge: 2007. Print.

33. Cohen, L. Playful Parenting. Ballantine Books: 2001. Print.

34. Wipfler, P. Listening to Children: Special Time. Parents Leadership Institute. Palo Alto: 1988. Print.

35. Wipfler, P. (n.d.). Citing Websites. In Playlistening. Retrieved June 1, 2013, from http://www.handinhandparenting.org/news/56/64/Playlistening

36. Val-Essen, I. Bring Out the Best in Your Child and Your Self. Quality Parenting: 2010. Print.

37. Sietsema, L. Personal Communication. May 2013.

38. Faber, A. & Mazlish, E. How To Talk So Kids Will Listen & Listen So Kids Will Talk. A division of Simon & Schuster, Inc. February 2012.

39. Steiner, R. (1919). Citing Websites. In Wikipedia. Retrieved June 4, 2013, from http://en.wikipedia.org/wiki/Waldorf_Education

40. Hicks, J. (April 9, 2011). Citing Websites. In Family Love Village blog. Retrieved June 4, 2013, from http://familylovevillage.blogspot.com/2011_05_01_archive.html

41. Beaglehole, R. (1999). Citing Websites. In Echo Parenting. Retrieved June 4, 2013, from http://www.echoparenting.org/parenting-programs

42. Hicks, J. (July 26, 2012). Citing Websites. In Family Love Village. Retrieved May 23, 2013, from http://familylovevillage.com/2012/07/4-steps-to-helping-your-child-transition-easefully/

43. VerDarLuz. Codex of the Soul: Astrology, Archetypes, and Your Sacred Blueprint. North Atlantic Books. Berkeley: 2012.

44. Newsom, J. Siebel (2011 & 2015). Citing Websites. In The Representation Project. Retrieved November 26, 2016, from http://therepresentationproject.org

45. Haggis, P. (2011). Citing Documentary. Retrieved November 26, 2016 from the film, Miss Representation

46. Couric, K. (2011). Citing Documentary. Retrieved November 26, 2016 from the film, Miss Representation

47. Kasl, C. (n.d.). Citing Websites. In Brainy Quote. Retrieved May 30, 2013, from http://www.brainyquote.com/quotes/authors/c/charlotte_davis_kasl.html

48. Kohn, A. (January 18, 1997). Citing Websites. In Carrots or Sticks? Alfie Kohn on Rewards and Punishments. Retrieved June 13, 2012, from http://www.alfiekohn.org/teaching/cktrots.htm

49. Zoghi, A. (2011, quoted in Truth of the Day. Book 1, by Amir Zoghi and the Universe, 2011)

50. Sage, C. Midwinter Turns to Spring. Think-Outside-the-Book Publishin, Inc. Beverly Hills: 2005. Print.

51. Kleinhans, J. (March 8, 2013). Citing Websites. In Family Love Village. http://familylovevillage.com/2013/03/the-importance-of-raising-children-with-an-abundant-mindset/

52. Zoghi, A. OMG (Oneness Mentorship Group) Workshop. September 2012. www.befreepeople.com

53. Barone, M. Citing Websites. In Family Love Village. Retrieved February 2013. http://familylovevillage.com/2013/02/living-and-learning-with-young-children/

54. Byrd, D. Personal communication. April 18, 2013. http://davidbyrdconsulting.com

55. C. Leo. Personal communication. April 24, 2013

56. Achor, S. Personal communication. April 20, 2013. http://goodthinkinc.com

57. Darwin, C. and Williams, J. (April 1998). Citing Websites. In Web Psych. Retrieved June 5, 2013, from http://web.psych.ualberta.ca/~varn/bc/Kleinke.htm

58. Ghandi, M. (n.d.). Citing Websites. In Brainy Quotes. Retrieved June 5, 2013, from http://www.brainyquote.com/quotes/authors/m/mahatma_gandhi.html

59. Wipfler, P. (n.d.). Citing Websites. In Hand in Hand Parenting. Retrieved June 5, 2013, from http://www.handinhandparenting.org/about-us

60. Hicks, J. (July 26, 2012). Citing Websites. In Family Love Village. Retrieved May 23, 2013, from http://familylovevillage.com/2012/07/4-steps-to-helping-your-child-transition-easefully/

61. Emoto, M. (July 25, 1999). Citing Websites. In Masaru Emoto. Retrieved June 5, 2013, from http://www.masaru-emoto.net/english/hado.html

ABOUT THE AUTHOR

Tangee Veloso, Founder and Executive Director of Family Love Village (FLV), is an eco-mamapreneur, an author and life and confidence coach who specializes in conscious co-parenting. Her mission is to empower co-parents to empathetically communicate while raising connected and confident children. Her commitment to bringing community together with the focus and awareness around conscious and sustainable living and compassionate parenting through connection has become an ever-evolving passion.

She is also the co-founder of another wonderful conscious community, A Thread of Connection (ATOC), that supports families with developing deeper relationships with their loved ones based on mutual respect and authentic communication. ATOC's main vision is to help parents/caregivers grow and become their best selves - all the while helping their children to discover their best selves, too!

Tangee has written many articles on finding ways to connect with our loved ones, our children, our planet, and just as importantly our connection to ourselves. She is also an experienced fire performer, spoken word artist, a loving mama to her son and a devoted ambassador of the concept with "being the change we wish to see in the world."

Tangee Veloso can be reached at:

tangee@tangeelifecoach.com

www.tangeelifecoach.com

www.ingramcontent.com/pod-product-compliance
Lightning Source LLC
Chambersburg PA
CBHW031146160426
43193CB00008B/270